P9-DVN-110

Delicious Barbecue & Microwave Recipes

ALPHA PUBLISHING™
A DIVISION OF ALPHA CORPORATION

325 DELICIOUS BARBECUE & MICROWAVE RECIPES

AN ALPHA PUBLISHING™ COOK BOOK

*This Premium Book features
Better Homes and Gardens
All-Time Favorite Barbecue Recipes
and selected recipes from
Richard Deacon's Microwave Cookery.*

BETTER HOMES AND GARDENS®
ALL-TIME FAVORITE BARBECUE RECIPES

A Bantam Book/published by arrangement with Meredith Corp. Copyright © 1995, 1992 by Meredith Corporation. For information address: Meredith Corporation, 1716 Locust Street, Des Moines, Iowa 50336

RICHARD DEACON'S MICROWAVE COOKERY
A Bantam Book/published by arrangement with
H.P Books, a division of the Putnam Berkley Group, Inc. Copyright ©
1995, 1977. For information address
Berkley Publishing Group, 200 Madison Avenue,
New York, NY 10016

Printed in the United States of America

For information on this special edition contact
Alpha Publishing,™
151 Bloor Street West, Suite 890,
Toronto,Ontario, Canada M5S 1S4

This special edition distributed exclusively by the Hudson's Bay Company in commemoration of their 325th Anniversary.

ISBN 1-896391-00-1

CONTENTS

BARBECUE RECIPES

GRILLING OVER THE COALS

Type of food	Cut or portion (placed 4 inches above coals)	Weight or thickness	Temperature of coals*
Beef	Burgers	½ inch	Medium-hot Medium
		¾ inch	Medium-hot Medium
	Porterhouse, T-bone, or sirloin steak	1 inch 1½ inches	Medium-hot Medium-hot Medium
	Chuck blade steak	1 inch 2½ inches	Medium Medium
Lamb	Rib chops	1 inch	Medium
		1½ inches	Medium
	Shoulder chops	1 inch	Medium
		1½ inches	Medium
Pork	Loin chops	1 inch 1½ inches	Medium Medium
	Blade steak	¾ inch	Medium
	Loin back ribs or spare ribs	5-6 pounds	Medium
Ham	Fully cooked slice	½ inch 1 inch	Medium-hot Medium
	Canned	5 pounds	Medium
Chicken	Broiler-fryer halves	2½-3 pounds	Medium-hot
	Roasting chicken, unstuffed	3-4 pounds	Medium
Turkey	Unstuffed	6-8 pounds	Medium
		12-16 pounds	Medium
Fish	Salmon or halibut steaks	¾ inch 1-1½ inches	Medium Medium-hot
	Trout, snapper, or whitefish fillets	6-8 ounces each	Medium-hot Medium
Seafood	Shrimp (large)	2 pounds	Hot

* Estimate by holding hand, palm down, about 4 inches above hot coals. Count seconds you can hold position. Figure 2 seconds as Hot coals; 3 seconds for Medium-hot coals. 4 seconds for Medium coals, and 5 or 6 seconds for Slow coals.

A handy guide for barbecuing your favorite foods

Approximate total cooking times				Comments
Open grill		Covered grill		
Rare	Medium	Rare	Medium	
8–10 min	10–12 min	7–9 min	8–10 min	Four burgers per pound
10–12 min	12–15 min	8–10 min	10–12 min	
10–12 min	12–15 min	8–10 min	10–12 min	Three burgers per pound
12–15 min	14–18 min	10–12 min	12–15 min	
12–18 min	15–20 min	8–10 min	10–15 min	Check doneness by cutting a slit in meat near bone
18–20 min	20–25 min	10–15 min	15–18 min	
20–25 min	25–30 min	15–18 min	18–22 min	
12–18 min	15–20 min	8–10 min	12–18 min	
50–60 min	55–65 min	45–55 min	50–60 min	Use foil tent on open grill
	20–25 min		20–25 min	Check doneness by cutting a slit in meat near bone
25–30 min	28–32 min	20–25 min	23–28 min	
	22–28 min		18–22 min	
28–32 min	30–35 min	20–25 min	25–30 min	
	Well-done		Well-done	
	22–25 min		18–22 min	A wire grill basket aids in turning
	30–35 min		25–30 min	
	15–20 min		15–20 min	
			1¼–1½ h	
	10–15 min		10–15 min	Slash fat edge of ham slice
	25–35 min		20–30 min	
	1½–1¾ h		1¼–1¾ h	Use foil tent on open grill
	45–50 min		40–45 min	
			2–2½ h	
			3–3¾ h	Meat thermometer inserted in thigh should register 185°
			3½–4½ h	
	17–22 min		15–20 min	Use a wire grill basket
	10–17 min		10–15 min	
	10–17 min		10–15 min	Use a wire grill basket
	17–20 min		15–17 min	
	15–18 min		15–18 min	

ROTISSERIE SPECIALTIES

Type of food	Cut	Weight	Temperature of coals*
Beef	Rolled rib roast	5-6 pounds	Medium
	Tenderloin roast	2½ pounds	Medium-hot
	Eye of round	3-4 pounds	Medium-hot
	Boneless rump roast	3-4 pounds	Slow
Lamb	Leg	5-7 pounds	Medium
Pork	Boneless loin roast	5-6 pounds	Medium
	Loin back ribs or spareribs	3-4 pounds	Slow
Ham	Boneless piece	9-10 pounds	Medium
	Canned	5 pounds	Medium
Chicken	Whole	2½-3 pounds	Medium-hot
			Medium
Cornish Hens	4 birds	1-1½ pounds	Medium-hot
Duckling	Whole domestic	4-6 pounds	Medium-hot
Turkey	Unstuffed	6-8 pounds	Medium
	2 rolled turkey roasts	28 ounces each	Medium-hot
	Boneless turkey roast	5-6 pounds	Medium-hot

SMOKER COOKING

Type of food	Cut or portion	Size or weight
Pork	Boneless loin roast	4-5 pounds
	6-8 loin chops	1½ inches thick (1 pound each)
	Loin back ribs or spareribs	4-5 pounds
Turkey	Ready-to-cook frozen bird, completely thawed	12-15 pounds
Fish	salmon (fillets or red snapper)	3-4 pounds

* Estimate by holding hand, palm down, about 4 inches above hot coals. Count seconds you can hold position. Figure 2 seconds as Hot coals; 3 seconds for Medium-hot coals; 4 seconds for Medium coals, and 5 or 6 seconds for Slow coals.

Guidelines for cooking meats and poultry on a spit

Approximate roasting time			Comments
Covered grill			
Rare	Medium	Well-done	
2–2½ hrs.	2½–3 hrs.		
40–45 min.	45–50 min.		
1¼–1½ hrs.	1½–2 hrs.		
	1¼–1¾ hrs.	1½–2 hrs.	Have meat rolled and tied
1 hr.	1½–2 hrs.	1¾–2¼ hrs.	Have shank cut off short / Balance diagonally on spit
		4–4½ hrs.	Have meat rolled and tied
		1–1¼ hrs.	Thread on spit accordion fashion
		2–2¼ hrs.	
		1¼–1½ hrs.	Tie securely after mounting on spit
		1½–1¾ hrs.	
		1½–2 hrs.	
		1½–1¾ hrs.	
		1½–1¾ hrs.	Deep foil drip pan is essential
		3¼–4½ hrs.	Push holding forks deep in bird
		1¾–2¼ hrs.	Purchase frozen; thaw completely
		2½–3½ hrs.	

Approximate timings when using a portable smoker°°

Approximate smoking time	Cuisson	Comments
4–5 hrs.	Well-done	170° on roast meat thermometer
2–2½ hrs.	Well-done	Cut slit in chop near bone to check doneness of meat
4–5 hrs.	Well-done	
8–9 hrs.	185° (internal temperature)	Check internal temperature at thigh with meat thermometer
2–3 hrs.	Well-done	Fish will flake easily with a fork

°°Check manufacturer's directions for placement of charcoal, hickory chips, and water pan.

BARBECUING
FOR EVERYONE

Getting superb results each time you barbecue—and enjoying your success—is what this book is all about. We've gathered recipes representing the best of barbecuing over the years. Enjoy sizzling steaks, ribs, grilled vegetables and breads, and savory desserts. Whether you're an experienced barbecue enthusiast or a "sometimes backyard chef," you'll find these Barbecue Recipes take the guesswork out of barbecuing.

MAIN DISHES FOR
OUTDOOR BARBECUES

If you've ever been tantalized by the smell of steaks, burgers, frankfurters, or other meats wafting through the air, you'll find much to be glad about in this section. In addition to scrumptious recipes for over-the-coals favorites, you'll discover new taste delights, too—beef short ribs, pork loin roasts, Cornish hens, salmon steaks, and many more. Try out your barbecuing skills at grilling, spit-roasting, skewer, or smoke cooking.

Beef

STEAK AND BACON TOURNEDOS

- 1 1- to 1½-pound beef flank steak
  Instant unseasoned meat
    tenderizer
- 10 slices bacon
- 1 teaspoon garlic salt
- ½ teaspoon freshly ground pepper
- 2 tablespoons snipped parsley
- 1 1¾-ounce envelope hollandaise
    sauce mix
- ¼ teaspoon dried tarragon,
    crushed

Pound flank steak evenly about ½ inch thick. Apply meat tenderizer according to package directions. Meanwhile, cook bacon till almost done, but not crisp.

Sprinkle flank steak with garlic salt and pepper. Score steak diagonally, making diamond-shaped cuts. Place bacon strips lengthwise on flank steak. Sprinkle with parsley. Roll up as for jelly roll, starting at narrow end. Skewer with wooden picks at 1-inch intervals. Cut into eight 1-inch slices with serrated knife.

Grill over *medium* coals for 8 minutes. Turn; grill 7 minutes more for rare. Meanwhile, in saucepan prepare hollandaise sauce mix according to package directions, adding tarragon to dry mix. Remove picks from meat slices. Serve hollandaise sauce with meat. Makes 4 servings.

VEGETABLE-BEEF ROLLS

 1 beaten egg
1½ pounds ground beef
 ½ cup shredded carrot
 ¼ cup finely chopped onion
 ¼ cup finely chopped green
      pepper
 ¼ cup finely chopped celery
 ½ teaspoon salt
     Dash pepper
12 slices bacon
 ½ cup Italian salad dressing

Combine egg and ground beef; mix well. Divide meat mixture into six portions. On waxed paper flatten each meat portion into a 6x4-inch rectangle. Combine carrot, onion, green pepper, celery, salt, and pepper. Divide vegetable mixture into six portions. Pat one vegetable portion onto each meat rectangle. Roll up each rectangle as for jelly roll. Wrap two slices of bacon around each of the rolls and secure with wooden picks.

Place rolls in shallow baking dish. Pour salad dressing over; let stand at room temperature about 1 hour, turning occasionally to moisten all sides. Remove meat rolls from dressing, reserving marinade. Grill rolls over *medium* coals for 20 to 25 minutes, turning to grill all sides and brushing with reserved dressing occasionally. Remove picks before serving. Makes 6 servings.

LEMON PEPPER FLANK PINWHEELS

2 1-pound beef flank steaks
½ cup Burgundy
¼ cup cooking oil
¼ cup soy sauce
1 tablespoon lemon pepper
1 tablespoon Worcestershire sauce
   Few drops bottled hot pepper
     sauce
8 cherry tomatoes *or* mushroom
     caps

Pound each flank steak to a 10x8-inch rectangle. Cut each rectangle into four 10x2-inch strips.

In bowl combine Burgundy, cooking oil, soy sauce, lemon pepper, Worcestershire, and pepper sauce. Place meat strips in plastic bag; set in a deep bowl. Pour wine mixture over meat; close bag. Marinate 4 to 6 hours or overnight in refrigerator, turning twice.

Drain meat; reserve marinade. Loosely roll each strip around a cherry tomato or mushroom cap, starting with short side. Skewer securely with wooden picks.

Grill pinwheels over *medium* coals for 15 minutes. Turn meat; grill about 10 minutes more for rare. Baste with marinade often. Remove picks. Makes 8 servings.

SMOKED FRENCH PEPPER STEAK

    Hickory chips
2   tablespoons cracked pepper
1   2-pound beef sirloin steak, cut 1½
        inches thick
¼   cup butter *or* margarine
2   tablespoons lemon juice
1   teaspoon Worcestershire sauce
½   teaspoon garlic powder
¼   teaspoon salt

About an hour before cooking time, soak hickory chips in enough water to cover. Drain.

Press cracked pepper into both sides of steak, using the heel of your hand or the flat side of a cleaver.

In saucepan over coals melt butter; stir in lemon juice, Worcestershire, garlic powder, and salt. Remove from coals.

Add damp hickory chips to *medium-hot* coals; place steak on grill and lower smoke hood. Grill steak for 17 to 20 minutes, brushing occasionally with lemon juice. Turn meat; grill, covered, 15 to 17 minutes more for rare to medium-rare. Heat reserved lemon sauce. Slice steak; spoon sauce over slices. Makes 6 servings.

PEPPY CHUCK STEAK GRILL

1 2- to 3-pound beef chuck steak,
    cut 1 inch thick
½ cup cooking oil
½ cut dry red wine
2 tablespoons catsup
2 tablespoons molasses
2 tablespoons finely snipped
    candied ginger
1 clove garlic, minced
1 teaspoon salt
¼ teaspoon pepper

Slash fat edges of steak, being careful not to cut into meat.
Place in shallow baking dish. Combine cooking oil, wine,
catsup, molasses, ginger, garlic, salt, and pepper. Pour over
steak. Cover; let stand 3 hours at room temperature or 6
hours, in refrigerator, turning several times.

Drain steak, reserving marinade. Pat excess moisture
from steak with paper toweling.

Grill steak over *medium* coals for about 20 minutes on
each side for rare; about 25 minutes on each side for
medium-rare. Brush occasionally with reserved marinade.

Remove meat to serving platter. Carve across grain in
thin slices. Makes 4 to 6 servings.

LEMON-MARINATED CHUCK ROAST

1 4-pound beef chuck pot roast,
    cut 1½ inches thick
1 teaspoon grated lemon peel
½ cup lemon juice
⅓ cup cooking oil
2 tablespoons sliced green onion
    with tops
4 teaspoons sugar
1½ teaspoons salt
1 teaspoon Worcestershire sauce
1 teaspoon prepared mustard
⅛ teaspoon pepper

Score fat edges of roast. Place meat in shallow baking dish. Combine lemon peel and juice, cooking oil, green onion, sugar, salt, Worcestershire, mustard, and pepper. Pour over roast. Cover; let stand 3 hours at room temperature or overnight in the refrigerator, turning roast several times.

Remove roast from marinade, reserving marinade. Pat excess moisture from roast with paper toweling.

Grill roast over *medium-hot* coals 17 to 20 minutes. Turn; cook 17 to 20 minutes more for rare to medium-rare. Heat reserved marinade on grill.

Remove roast to serving platter. Carve across the grain into thin slices. Spoon marinade over. Serves 6 to 8.

ONION-STUFFED STEAK

2 1¼- to 1½-pound porterhouse
      steaks, cut 1½ inches thick *or* 1
      2-pound sirloin steak, cut 1½
      inches thick
½ cup chopped onion
1 large clove garlic, minced
1 tablespoon butter *or* margarine
   Dash celery salt
   Dash pepper
¼ cup dry red wine
2 tablespoons soy sauce
1 cup sliced fresh mushrooms
2 tablespoons butter *or* margarine

Slash fat edges of steak at 1-inch intervals, being careful
not to cut into meat. Slice pockets in each side of meat,
cutting almost to bone.

In skillet cook onion and garlic in the 1 tablespoon butter. Add celery salt and pepper. Stuff pockets with onion
mixture; skewer closed. Mix wine and soy sauce; brush on
steak. Grill over *medium-hot* coals for 15 minutes; brush
often with soy mixture. Turn; grill 10 to 15 minutes more
for rare. Brush often with soy mixture. In small skillet cook
mushrooms in the 2 tablespoons butter till tender. Slice
steak across grain; pass the mushrooms and spoon atop
steak. Makes 4 servings.

RICE-STUFFED FLANK STEAK

1 1- to 1¼-pound beef flank steak
½ teaspoon unseasoned meat
      tenderizer
¼ cup chopped onion
¼ cup chopped celery
2 tablespoons butter *or* margarine
½ cup water
1 tablespoon curry powder
1 teaspoon instant beef bouillon
      granules
¼ cup quick-cooking rice

Score meat diagonally on both sides; pound to an 11x9-inch rectangle. Sprinkle with tenderizer, salt, and pepper.

In saucepan cook onion and celery in butter till tender. Add water, curry, and bouillon; stir in rice. Bring to boiling; cover. Remove from heat: let stand 5 minutes.

Spread mixture on meat; roll up as for jelly roll, starting at short side. Tie with string both lengthwise and crosswise.

Insert spit rod lengthwise through center of steak. Adjust holding forks; test balance. Place *medium* coals on both sides of drip pan. Attach spit; position drip pan under meat. Turn on motor: lower hood or cover with foil tent. Toast over *medium* coals till done, about 50 minutes. Remove strings. Makes 4 servings.

SPIT-ROASTED CHATEAUBRIAND

1 2- to 2½ pound beef tenderloin
1 cup crumbled blue cheese
       (4 ounces)
1 tablespoon brandy

Trim fat from surface of roast. Make a slanting cut, 2 inches deep, the full length of the roast with a sharp, narrow-bladed knife held at a 45-degree angle. Make another cut, just as before, along opposite side.

Blend blue cheese and brandy together. Spread cheese mixture in the two slashed openings. Securely tie string around the roast at both ends and the middle.

Insert spit rod lengthwise through center of roast. Adjust holding forks; test balance. Insert meat thermometer near center of roast, not touching metal rod. Place *hot* coals on both sides of drip pan. Attach spit; position drip pan under meat. Turn on motor; lower hood or cover with foil tent. Grill over *hot* coals till thermometer registers 130° for rare (about 45 minutes), 150° for medium-rare (about 50 minutes), and 160° for medium-medium well (55 to 60 minutes). Remove string. Makes 6 to 8 servings.

MARINATED HICKORY-SMOKED CHUCK ROAST

1   2-pound beef chuck pot roast,
        cut 1¼ inches thick
5   cloves garlic, peeled
¼   cup cooking oil
¼   cup wine vinegar
1   tablespoon Worcestershire sauce
½   teaspoon salt
½   teaspoon dried basil, crushed
¼   teaspoon pepper
     Several dashes bottled hot
        pepper sauce
     Hickory chips

Stud roast with garlic by inserting tip of knife in meat and pushing cloves into meat as you remove knife. Make sure garlic cloves are evenly spaced.

In bowl mix oil, vinegar, Worcestershire, salt, basil, pepper, and hot pepper sauce. Place meat in plastic bag; set in shallow baking dish. Pour marinade over meat; close bag. Marinate 6 to 8 hours or overnight in refrigerator; turning roast occasionally.

About an hour before cooking soak hickory chips in enough water to cover; drain chips. Drain meat, reserving marinade. Pat excess moisture from meat with paper toweling. Arrange *medium-slow* coals around drip pan. Add hickory chips to coals. Place roast over drip pan on grill. Lower hood. Grill 25 minutes. Brush occasionally with marinade and add additional hickory chips. Turn roast; grill 20 minutes more for medium, brushing with marinade. Season to taste; remove garlic. Serves 6.

RIB ROAST BARBECUE

1 5- to 6-pound boned and rolled
   beef rib roast
½ cup Burgundy
½ cup vinegar
¼ cup cooking oil
¼ cup finely chopped onion
2 tablespoons sugar
1 tablespoon Worcestershire
   sauce
1½ teaspoons salt
½ teaspoon dry mustard
¼ teaspoon pepper
¼ teaspoon chili powder
¼ teaspoon dried thyme, crushed
1 clove garlic, minced
   Several drops bottled hot
   pepper sauce

Place meat in plastic bag; set in deep bowl. Combine remaining ingredients. Pour over meat; close bag. Marinate 6 to 8 hours or overnight in refrigerator; turn several times.

Drain meat; reserve marinade. Pat excess moisture from meat with paper toweling. Insert spit rod through center of roast. Adjust holding forks; test balance. insert meat thermometer near center of roast but not touching metal rod. Place *medium* coals around drip pan. Attach spit; position drip pan under meat. Turn on motor; lower hood or cover with foil tent. Roast over *medium* coals till meat thermometer registers 140° for rare (2 to 2½ hours), 160° for medium, and 170° for well-done. Brush frequently with marinade during the last 30 minutes of roasting. Let stand 15 minutes before slicing. If desired, heat remaining marinade and pass with meat. Makes 15 to 20 servings.

HOT-STYLE EYE OF ROUND

1 3-pound beef eye of round roast
   Instant unseasoned meat
      tenderizer
1 cup hot-style catsup
½ cup water
2 tablespoons Worcestershire sauce
1 clove garlic, minced
½ teaspoon chili powder
¼ teaspoon salt

Sprinkle all sides of roast evenly with tenderizer, using ½ teaspoon per pound of meat. To ensure penetration, pierce all sides deeply at ½-inch intervals with long-tined fork. In saucepan combine catsup, water, Worcestershire, garlic, chili powder, and salt. Simmer 5 minutes.

Insert spit rod through center of roast. Adjust holding forks; test balance. insert meat thermometer near center of roast, not touching metal rod. Place *medium-hot* coals around drip pan. Attach spit; position drip pan under meat. Turn on motor; lower hood or cover with foil tent. Roast over *medium-hot* coals till thermometer registers 140° for rare, about 1½ hours. Brush with sauce during last 30 minutes. Heat sauce; pass with meat. Serves 8.

CORNED BEEF BARBECUE DINNER

1 3-pound piece corned beef for
     oven roasting
6 medium baking potatoes
1 envelope dry onion soup mix
½ cup butter *or* margarine,
     softened
½ cup sugar
¼ cup vinegar
3 tablespoons prepared mustard
     Dash salt
1 cup dairy sour cream
¼ cup milk
2 tablespoons prepared mustard

Unwrap and rinse corned beef. Arrange *medium* coals around edge of grill. Place beef on heavy-duty foil drip pan on grill. Close hood; grill for 1½ hours. Scrub potatoes but do not peel. Cut each in 3 or 4 lengthwise slices. Set aside 3 tablespoons soup mix. Blend together remaining soup mix and butter. Spread mixture over potato slices. Reassemble potatoes. Wrap each in a square of the heavy-duty foil. Place at edges of grill. Grill, hood down, along with meat for 45 to 60 minutes more; turn potatoes once.

Meanwhile, in saucepan mix sugar, vinegar, 3 tablespoons mustard, and salt. Bring to boiling; stir till sugar dissolves. Brush over meat during last few minutes of grilling. Just before serving, mix sour cream, milk, reserved soup mix, and 2 tablespoons mustard. Heat through, stirring occasionally. *Do not boil*.

Unwrap potatoes. Arrange meat and potatoes on serving platter. Serve with sour cream sauce. Makes 6 servings.

BRAZILIAN BARBECUED BEEF

1 4-pound beef chuck pot roast,
       cut 2 to 2½ inches thick
1 cup catsup
⅓ cup vinegar
¼ cup cooking oil
2 tablespoons instant coffee
       crystals
1 teaspoon salt
1 teaspoon chili powder
1 teaspoon celery seed
½ teaspoon pepper
⅛ teaspoon garlic powder
3 or 4 dashes bottled hot pepper
       sauce

Slash fat edges of meat, being careful not to cut into meat.
Place roast in shallow baking dish. In small bowl combine
catsup, vinegar, oil, coffee crystals, salt, chili powder, celery seed, pepper, garlic powder, hot pepper sauce, and ½
cup water; pour over roast. Cover; refrigerate 6 to 8 hours
or overnight, turning roast several times. Remove roast
from marinade, reserving marinade. Remove excess moisture from roast with paper toweling. Grill roast over
medium coals for 20 to 25 minutes. Turn roast; grill 10
minutes. Brush roast with marinade. Grill for 10 to 15 minutes more for rare to medium rare, brushing occasionally
with marinade. Heat remaining marinade.

To serve, carve meat across the grain in thin slices. Pass
heated marinade. Makes 6 to 8 servings.

WINED-AND-DINED BEEF ROAST

1 clove garlic, minced
3 tablespoons cooking oil
½ cup dry red wine
2 tablespoons lemon juice
1 teaspoon dried basil, crushed
½ teaspoon dry mustard
1 3-pound beef chuck pot roast,
    cut 1½ inches thick
2 tablespoons bottled steak sauce

Cook garlic in oil; remove from heat. Add wine, lemon juice, basil, dry mustard, and ½ teaspoon salt. Prick roast on both sides with long-tined fork; place in plastic bag and set in deep bowl. Pour in marinade; close bag. Marinate overnight in refrigerator, turning roast in bag or pressing marinade against roast occasionally. Drain meat, reserving marinade. Remove excess moisture from roast with paper toweling. Add steak sauce to reserved marinade. Grill over *medium* coals 25 to 30 minutes on each side for medium doneness. Brush with marinade. Serves 6 to 8.

Avoid Flare-Ups
with a Drip Pan

When grilling large pieces of meat, use a drip pan to catch meat juices. Make your own pan as follows: (A) Tear off a piece of 18-inch-wide heavy-duty foil twice the length of your grill and fold it in half for a double thickness. Turn up all edges of the foil 1½ inches. (B) Miter corners securely and fold tips toward the inside for added strength. (C) Set the drip pan under the meat to catch drippings, and arrange the coals around the pan. Position the pan in place either before or after you ignite the charcoal. Carefully empty the drip pan after each use.

HORSERADISH-STUFFED RUMP ROAST

¼ cup prepared horseradish
2 cloves garlic, minced
1 5-pound boneless beef rump
    roast, rolled and tied
1 clove garlic, halved

Combine horseradish and minced garlic. Unroll roast;
make a lengthwise cut slightly off-center going almost to
but not through other side. (Leave center area uncut for
spit to go through.) Spread cut area with horseradish mixture. Reroll roast and tie securely. Insert spit rod through
center of roast. Adjust holding forks; test balance. Rub outside of roast with the additional clove of garlic. Insert meat
thermometer. Place *medium* coals on both sides of drip
pan. Attach spit; position drip pan under meat. Turn on
motor; lower hood or cover with foil tent. Roast till thermometer registers 140° for medium-rare, about 1½ hours.
Let stand 15 minutes before carving. Serves 10.

WINE-BASTED SHORT RIBS

½ cup dry red wine
1 teaspoon dried thyme, crushed
½ teaspoon garlic salt
½ teaspoon lemon pepper
2 pounds beef plate short ribs, cut
    in serving-size pieces

In large Dutch oven combine wine, thyme, garlic salt,
lemon pepper, and ½ cup water. Add rib pieces. Cover and
simmer just till tender, 1¼ to 1½ hours. Drain, reserving
liquid. Place ribs over *slow* coals. Grill till done, 15 to 20
minutes, turning ribs occasionally and brushing with wine
mixture. Makes 4 servings.

SMOKED SHORT RIBS

Hickory chips
4 pounds beef plate short ribs, cut
    in serving-size pieces
1 10¾-ounce can condensed tomato
    soup
¾ cup dry red wine
¼ cup finely chopped onion
2 tablespoons cooking oil
1 tablespoon prepared mustard
2 teaspoons chili powder
1 teaspoon paprika
1 teaspoon celery seed
¼ teaspoon salt

Soak hickory chips in enough water to cover about an hour before cooking time. Drain chips. In covered grill place *slow* coals on both sides of drip pan. Sprinkle coals with some dampened hickory chips. Place ribs, bone side down, on grill. Lower grill hood. Grill ribs till done, about 1½ hours, adding more hickory chips every 20 minutes.

Meanwhile, in saucepan mix tomato soup, wine, onion, cooking oil, mustard, chili powder, paprika, celery seed, and ¼ teaspoon salt. Heat sauce at side of grill. Brush ribs with sauce. Grill, uncovered, about 20 minutes more; brush ribs frequently with sauce. Serves 4 or 5.

Be Sure with a Meat Thermometer

Using a meat thermometer helps you make sure your roasts are cooked the way you want them—to perfection. Insert thermometer in center of raw roast so tip reaches thickest part of meat and does not touch fat, bone, or metal spit rod. When thermometer registers the doneness you like (see charts, pages 2-5), push it into meat a little farther. If temperature drops below the desired temperature, continue cooking till it rises again.

QUICK GARLIC CUBED STEAKS

¼ cup butter *or* margarine
2 tablespoons Worcestershire sauce
2 tablespoons lemon juice
1 teaspoon finely snipped parsley
½ teaspoon celery salt
1 clove garlic, minced
6 beef cubed steaks
6 Vienna *or* French bread slices,
    toasted

In saucepan melt butter or margarine; stir in Worcestershire sauce, lemon juice, snipped parsley, celery salt, and garlic. Brush butter mixture on both sides of steaks. Place the steaks in wire grill basket. Grill over *hot* coals for 1 to 2 minutes. Turn basket over and grill for 1 to 2 minutes more. Season steaks with salt and pepper. Place each steak atop a slice of toasted bread. Spoon remaining butter mixture over steaks. Serves 6.

BEEF AND BEAN RAGOUT

    2 tablespoons cooking oil
    2 pounds beef for stew, cut in ½-
        inch pieces
 3½ cups water
    3 medium potatoes, peeled and
        cubed (3 cups)
    2 cups chopped peeled tomatoes
        or 1 16-ounce can tomatoes,
        cut up
    2 medium onions, chopped
    1 6-ounce can tomato paste
    1 medium green pepper, chopped
    ¼ cup snipped parsley
    1 tablespoon instant beef bouillon
        granules
 1½ teaspoons salt
    1 teaspoon sugar
    ½ teaspoon dried basil, crushed
    ½ teaspoon dried thyme, crushed
    ¼ teaspoon pepper
    1 bay leaf
    1 15½-ounce can red kidney
        beans, drained
    ¾ cup dry red wine
    ¼ cup all-purpose flour

Heat oil in heavy 4-quart Dutch oven over *hot* coals;
brown half the meat at a time in the hot oil. Add 3 *cups* of
the water, potatoes, tomatoes, onions, tomato paste, green
pepper, parsley, beef bouillon granules, and seasonings.
Cover and heat to boiling (will take about 1¼ hours), stirring occasionally. Add coals as necessary. Boil till meat and
vegetables are tender, about 1 hour more, stirring occasionally. Stir in beans and wine. Cover and heat to boiling.
Blend the remaining ½ cup water into the flour; stir into
bean mixture. Cook, stirring constantly, till mixture thickens and bubbles. Remove bay leaf. Makes 6 servings.

SMOKED BEEF AND CHEESE SOUP

4 cups milk
1 10¾-ounce can cream of potato
    soup
1 4-ounce package sliced smoked
    beef, snipped (1 cup)
1 cup shredded Muenster cheese
¼ cup finely chopped onion
2 tablespoons snipped parsley
½ teaspoon caraway seed

In heavy 3-quart saucepan gradually stir milk into soup. Add smoked beef, cheese, onion, parsley, and caraway seed. Cook and stir over *hot* coals till mixture is heated through, about 30 minutes, stirring often. Serves 6 to 8.

BEEF AND MUSHROOM KABOBS

½ cup cooking oil
⅓ cup soy sauce
¼ cup lemon juice
2 tablespoons prepared mustard
2 tablespoons Worcestershire
    sauce
1 clove garlic, minced
1 teaspoon coarsely cracked
    pepper
1½ teaspoons salt
1½ pounds lean beef round *or*
    chuck, cut in 1-inch pieces
    Boiling water
12 to 16 mushroom caps

Mix oil, soy sauce, lemon juice, mustard, Worcestershire, garlic, pepper, and 1½ teaspoons salt. Add beef pieces. Cover and refrigerate overnight; turn meat occasionally. Pour boiling water over mushrooms. Let stand a few minutes; drain. Thread meat and mushrooms on skewers. Grill over *hot* coals till meat is desired doneness; allow 15 minutes for medium-rare; turn often. Makes 4 or 5 servings.

STEAK AND SHRIMP KABOB DINNER

½ cup catsup
¼ cup water
¼ cup finely chopped onion
1 tablespoon brown sugar
3 tablespoons lemon juice
2 tablespoons cooking oil
2 teaspoons prepared mustard
2 teaspoons Worcestershire sauce
½ teaspoon chili powder
1 pound beef sirloin steak, cut in 1-inch pieces
½ pound fresh *or* frozen shrimp, shelled
2 zucchini, cut diagonally in 1-inch pieces
2 ears corn, cut in 1-inch pieces
2 small onions, cut in wedges
1 green pepper *or* red sweet pepper, cut in squares
6 cherry tomatoes

In small saucepan combine catsup, water, chopped onion, and brown sugar. Stir in lemon juice, cooking oil, prepared mustard, Worcestershire sauce, and chili powder. Simmer, uncovered, 10 minutes, stirring once or twice.

On six short skewers thread steak pieces alternately with shrimp, zucchini, corn, onion wedges, and pepper squares. Grill kabobs over *medium-hot* coals till meat is desired doneness, allow 15 to 17 minutes for medium-rare. Turn kabobs often, brushing with sauce. Garnish end of each skewer with a cherry tomato. Makes 3 or 4 servings.

How to Turn Barbecued Steaks

Every time a drop of meat juice falls to its sizzling end on the coals, you're losing a little bit of the flavor that makes barbecued steak so delicious. To prevent this flavor loss, be sure to use tongs when turning the meat. Or, if you don't have tongs, insert a fork into a strip of fat and flip steak with a turner.

BEEF-YAM KABOBS

4   medium yams *or* sweet potatoes
      or 1 8-ounce can syrup-packed
      sweet potatoes
¼   cup packed brown sugar
1   teaspoon cornstarch
½   cup orange juice
¼   cup chili sauce
1   tablespoon prepared mustard
1   pound beef sirloin steak, cut ½
      inch thick
1   orange, cut into 8 wedges

Cut off woody portion of fresh yams or sweet potatoes. In saucepan cook fresh yams or sweet potatoes, covered, in enough boiling salted water to cover till potatoes are tender, 25 to 30 minutes. Drain; cool potatoes. Peel and cut into 1-inch pieces. (If using canned sweet potatoes, drain; cut sweet potatoes into 1-inch pieces.)

Meanwhile, prepare sauce. In small saucepan stir together brown sugar and cornstarch; stir in orange juice, chili sauce, and mustard. Cook, stirring constantly, till thickened and bubbly. Simmer, uncovered, 5 minutes; stirring once or twice. Sprinkle steak with salt and pepper; cut steak into 1-inch pieces. On four skewers alternately thread steak pieces, yam or sweet potato pieces, and orange wedges. Grill over *medium* coals till meat is desired doneness, allow 12 to 14 minutes for medium-rare. Turn kabobs occasionally and brush frequently with some of the sauce; pass remaining sauce. Makes 4 servings.

SKEWERED BEEF BUNDLES

⅛ cup soy sauce
2 tablespoons sugar
¼ teaspoon ground ginger
1 pound beef round tip steak, cut 1
    inch thick
½ pound fresh whole green beans
4 large carrots, cut into 3-inch-long
    sticks
2 tablespoons butter *or* margarine,
    melted

In medium bowl combine soy sauce, sugar, and ginger. Cut steak into thin strips. Cover; marinate meat in soy mixture for 2 to 3 hours at room temperature, stirring occasionally. Meanwhile, cook beans and carrots separately in boiling salted water till barely tender; drain well and cool. Wrap half the meat strips around bundles of four beans; repeat with remaining meat and carrot sticks. Secure with wooden picks. Thread bundles ladder fashion on two parallel skewers. Brush with melted butter. Grill over *medium* coals about 4 minutes. Turn and grill for 3 to 4 minutes more. Brush with melted butter once or twice more during cooking. Serves 4 or 5.

SKEWERED CHERRY TOMATO MEATBALLS

1 beaten egg
¾ cup soft bread crumbs (1 slice)
¼ cup milk
¾ cup finely chopped onion
¾ teaspoon salt
½ teaspoon dried oregano,
    crushed
⅛ teaspoon pepper
1 pound ground beef
15 cherry tomatoes
2 dill pickles, cut into ½-inch
    chunks
    Bottled steak sauce

In bowl combine egg, bread crumbs, milk, onion, salt,
oregano, and pepper. Add ground beef; mix well. Shape 3
tablespoons of the meat mixture around each cherry
tomato to form meatballs. On five large skewers thread
meatballs and dill pickle chunks. Grill over *medium* coals
for 15 to 20 minutes, turning 3 or 4 times to cook evenly;
brush meatballs occasionally with steak sauce. Makes 5
servings.

HAWAIIAN KABOBS

½ cup soy sauce
¼ cup cooking oil
1 tablespoon dark corn syrup
2 cloves garlic, minced
1 teaspoon dry mustard
1 teaspoon ground ginger
2½ pounds beef sirloin steak, cut in
    1½-inch pieces
3 green peppers, cut in 1-inch
    squares
5 small firm tomatoes, quartered

In large bowl combine soy sauce, oil, corn syrup, garlic, dry mustard, and ginger. Add meat; cover and refrigerate several hours or overnight. Drain meat, reserving marinade. Alternate meat, green pepper, and tomato on skewers. Grill over *medium-hot* coals till desired doneness, allow about 15 minutes for rare. Baste the kabobs occasionally with reserved marinade. Makes 8 servings.

Burgers and Sandwiches

BURGERS O'BRIEN

    1 12-ounce package frozen loose-
          pack hash brown potatoes (3
          cups)
    ¼ cup chopped onion
    ¼ cup chopped green pepper
    2 tablespoons melted butter
    1 beaten egg
    2 tablespoons chopped pimento
  1½ teaspoons salt
    ¼ teaspoon pepper
  1½ pounds ground beef
    8 hamburger buns, split, toasted,
          and buttered

Chop potatoes slightly; sprinkle with salt. In skillet combine potatoes, onion, green pepper, and butter. Cover and
cook till potatoes are tender, stirring occasionally.
Combine egg, pimento, 1½ teaspoons salt, and pepper; stir
in potato mixture. Add ground beef; mix well. Shape meat
mixture into 8 patties, about ½ inch thick. Grill over
medium-hot coals for 5 minutes. Turn and grill 3 to 4 minutes more. Serve patties on toasted buns; place green pepper ring atop burger, if desired. Serves 8.

BEEF AND CARROT BURGERS

1 beaten egg
2 tablespoons milk
¼ cup wheat germ
½ cup grated carrot
¼ cup finely chopped onion
¾ teaspoon salt
¼ teaspoon dried marjoram,
     crushed
⅛ teaspoon pepper
1 pound ground beef
4 slices Monterey Jack cheese
4 whole wheat hamburger buns,
     split, toasted, and buttered
4 lettuce leaves
4 tomato slices

Combine egg, milk, and wheat germ; stir in carrot, onion, salt, marjoram, and pepper. Add ground beef; mix well. Shape into four patties. Grill over *medium-hot* coals for 5 to 6 minutes; turn and grill 4 to 5 minutes more. During last minute of cooking time, place a slice of cheese atop each patty. Serve patties on toasted buns with lettuce and tomato. Makes 4 servings.

BURGERS EXTRAVAGANZA

    1 beaten egg
    ¼ cup water
    ¼ cup fine dry bread crumbs
    ¼ teaspoon dried oregano,
          crushed
    ¼ teaspoon fennel seed
    ¼ teaspoon garlic salt
    ¼ teaspoon onion salt
       Dash pepper
  1½ pounds ground beef
    ½ pound bulk pork sausage
    8 slices American cheese
    8 onion slices
    8 hamburger buns, split, toasted,
          and buttered

In bowl combine egg, water, bread crumbs, oregano, fennel, garlic salt, onion salt, and pepper. Add ground beef and sausage; mix well. Form into 8 patties, ½ inch thick. Grill burgers over *medium* coals for 6 to 7 minutes. Turn and cook 6 to 7 minutes more. Top each patty with a cheese and onion slice; serve on toasted buns. Makes 8 servings.

BACON BURGER SQUARES

    8 slices bacon
    2 pounds ground beef
    2 tablespoons lemon juice
    1 tablespoon Worcestershire sauce
       Salt
       Pepper
    8 hamburger buns, split and
          toasted

Cook bacon till almost done, but not crisp. Cut bacon strips in half crosswise. Pat ground beef to a 12x6-inch rectangle; cut into 8 squares. Combine lemon juice and Worcestershire; brush over the beef patties. Sprinkle with salt and pepper. Arrange squares in greased wire grill basket. Place 2 half-slices of bacon crisscrossed atop each burger to form an "X." Close basket. Grill burgers over *medium-hot* coals, turning often, till desired doneness, about 20 minutes. Serve on hamburger buns. Serves 8.

CHILI BURGER PATTIES

2½ pounds ground beef
¾ cup chili sauce
4 teaspoons prepared mustard
4 teaspoons prepared horseradish
4 teaspoons Worcestershire sauce
1 tablespoon chopped onion
2 teaspoons salt
  Dash pepper
12 hamburger buns, split and
    toasted

In mixing bowl thoroughly combine ground beef, chili sauce, prepared mustard, horseradish, Worcestershire sauce, chopped onion, salt, and pepper; mix well. Form into 12 patties. Grill over *medium-hot* coals for 5 minutes. Turn patties and grill till desired doneness, about 3 minutes longer. Serve grilled patties on hamburger buns. Serves 12.

BASIC GRILLED BURGERS

1 pound ground beef
½ teaspoon salt
  Dash pepper

Mix ground beef, salt, and pepper. Form into four 4-inch patties. Grill over *medium-hot* coals for 5 to 6 minutes; turn and grill 4 to 5 minutes more. Serves 4.

For Variations: Add any of the following to basic meat mixture; 2 tablespoons chopped green onion with tops; 2

tablespoons drained sweet pickle relish; 2 tablespoons chopped pimento-stuffed olives; 1 tablespoon prepared horseradish; or ¼ teaspoon instant minced garlic.

BARBECUED BEEF BURGERS

1 beaten egg
2 tablespoons milk
2 tablespoons catsup
¼ cup finely crushed saltine
    crackers (7 crackers)
½ teaspoon salt
1 pound ground beef
4 thin slices onion
4 slices sharp American cheese
¼ cup chopped onion
¼ cup butter *or* margarine
¼ cup catsup
2 tablespoons brown sugar
½ teaspoon prepared horseradish
½ teaspoon salt

Combine egg, milk, and 2 tablespoons catsup; stir in cracker crumbs and ½ teaspoon salt. Add ground beef; mix well. Form into four patties; place each on a 12-inch square of heavy-duty foil. Top each patty with 1 slice onion and 1 slice cheese.

Cook chopped onion in butter till tender but not brown. Add ¼ cup catsup, brown sugar, horseradish, and ½ teaspoon salt; simmer, uncovered, 5 minutes. Spoon over burgers. Wrap foil loosely around meat, sealing edges well. Cook the bundles over *medium* coals, onion side down, for 15 minutes. Turn burgers over; grill till desired doneness, about 10 minutes more. Makes 4 servings.

VEGETABLE BURGERS

2 slightly beaten eggs
¾ cup soft bread crumbs
¼ cup finely chopped onion
¼ cup catsup
1½ pounds ground beef
1 6-ounce can chopped
    mushrooms, drained
6 slices American cheese
6 hamburger buns
6 slices onion
6 slices tomato

In bowl combine eggs, crumbs, onion, catsup, 1 teaspoon salt, and dash pepper., Add beef; mix well. Form into 12 patties. Top *half* of the patties with mushrooms to within ¾ inch of edge. Top with remaining patties, sealing edges. Grill over *medium* coals for 5 to 6 minutes. Turn and grill till desired doneness, 5 to 6 minutes more. Top with cheese; heat just till melted. Split and toast hamburger buns. Serve burgers on buns with onion and tomato slices. Makes 6 servings.

CHEESE-STUFFED PATTIES

1 pound ground beef
½ teaspoon salt
  Dash pepper
  American cheese, shredded
  Chopped onion
  Bottled barbecue sauce

Mix ground beef, salt, and pepper. Between sheets of waxed paper, roll out patties ¼ inch thick. Center half of patties with small amount of cheese, onion, and barbecue sauce. Top with remaining meat patties; press around edges to seal. Grill over *medium-hot* coals about 7 minutes. Turn meat; grill 6 to 7 minutes more. Makes 3 burgers.

BURRITO BURGERS

1 cup refried beans (½ of 15-
   ounce can)
1 4-ounce can mild green chili
   peppers, drained, seeded, and
   chopped
¼ cup chopped onion
1½ pounds ground beef
4 slices sharp American cheese
8 flour tortillas
1 cup chopped lettuce
1 medium tomato, chopped

Combine beans, *2 tablespoons* of the chili peppers, onion, and ¾ teaspoon salt. Add beef; mix well. Form into eight 5-inch patties. Cut cheese slices in half; place ½ cheese slice on each beef patty. Fold to seal cheese inside, forming semicircle. Grill over *medium* coals for 5 to 6 minutes; turn and grill 4 to 5 minutes more. Heat the tortillas on grill. Serve burgers in hot tortillas. Add the lettuce, chopped tomato, and remaining chili peppers as desired. Makes 8 servings.

Don't Do without a Wire Grill Basket

Wire grill baskets are indispensable when you grill foods that need frequent turning or are difficult to turn, such as burgers, frankfurters, bite-size rib appetizers, chops, or shrimp. A hinged grill basket is the best buy, since you can adjust it to hold small fish, thick burgers, thin steaks, or chicken halves, quarters, or cut-up pieces.

MINI PINEAPPLE MEAT LOAVES

1 14¼-ounce can crushed
   pineapple (juice pack)
2 beaten eggs
1½ cups soft bread crumbs (2
   slices)
2 tablespoons finely chopped
   onion
2 tablespoons chopped green
   pepper
½ teaspoon salt
⅛ teaspoon pepper
1½ pounds ground beef
1 tablespoon cornstarch
2 teaspoons prepared mustard
¼ cup catsup
2 tablespoons soy sauce
4 drops bottled hot pepper sauce

Drain crushed pineapple; reserve juice. Add water to
juice, if necessary, to make 1 cup; set aside for use in sauce.
In bowl combine eggs, bread crumbs, pineapple, onion,
green pepper, salt, and pepper. Add beef; mix well. Form
into five 4x2-inch loaves. Place meat loaves in wire grill
basket. Grill over *medium-hot* coals for 20 to 25 minutes.
Turn and grill till done, about 20 minutes more.

Meanwhile, in small saucepan blend together cornstarch and mustard. Stir in reserved pineapple juice, catsup, soy sauce, and hot pepper sauce. Cook over *medium-
hot* coals, stirring constantly, till thickened and bubbly.
Pass with meat loaves. Makes 5 servings.

GIANT STUFFED GRILLBURGERS

    1 beaten egg
1¼ cup herb-seasoned stuffing mix,
       crushed
    1 4-ounce can chopped
       mushrooms, drained
  ⅓ cup beef broth
  ¼ cup sliced green onion with tops
  ¼ cup snipped parsley
    2 tablespoons butter *or*
       margarine, melted
    1 teaspoon lemon juice
    2 pounds ground beef
    1 teaspoon salt

Mix together the egg, stuffing mix, drained mushrooms, beef broth, green onion, parsley, butter or margarine, and lemon juice; set aside. Combine meat and salt; divide mixture in half. On sheets of waxed paper, pat each half to an 8-inch circle. Spoon stuffing over one circle of meat to within 1 inch of edge. Top with second circle of meat; peel off top sheet of paper and seal edges of meat.

Invert meat patty onto well-greased wire grill basket; peel off remaining paper. Grill over *medium* coals for 10 to 12 minutes. Turn and grill till desired doneness, 10 to 12 minutes more. Cut the burger into wedges; serve with warmed catsup, if desired. Makes 8 servings.

CHILI MEAT LOAF

  2 slightly beaten eggs
  1 8-ounce can tomatoes, cut up
  1 8-ounce can red kidney beans,
     drained
  1 cup crushed corn chips
  ¼ cup finely chopped green onion
     with tops
  2 tablespoons snipped parsley
 1½ teaspoons salt
  1 teaspoon chili powder
  2 pounds lean ground beef
  1 10-ounce can mild enchilada
     sauce
  ½ cup shredded sharp American
     cheese (2 ounces)

Combine eggs, undrained tomatoes, beans, corn chips, green onion, parsley, salt, and chili powder; mash beans slightly. Add ground beef; mix well. Shape into two 7x3x2-inch loaves. Tear off two 18-inch lengths of 18-inch-wide heavy-duty foil. Place loaves on foil pieces; wrap foil around each loaf and seal securely. Grill over *medium* coals 30 minutes. Turn and grill 20 minutes longer.

    Meanwhile, in saucepan heat enchilada sauce. Open foil and fold down to make "pan." Continue cooking meat till done, about 10 minutes more, brushing frequently with enchilada sauce. Pass remaining sauce and cheese to top each serving. Makes 8 servings.

STUFFED STEAK SANDWICHES

2 1-pound beef flank steaks
   Instant unseasoned meat
     tenderizer
2 tablespoons prepared
     horseradish
⅓ cup chopped onion
⅓ cup chopped celery
2 tablespoons butter *or*
     margarine, melted
½ teaspoon seasoned salt
1 cup dairy sour cream
12 slices French bread, toasted and
     buttered

Score steaks diagonally on both sides. Use tenderizer according to directions. Spread one side of steaks with horseradish. Combine onion, celery, butter, and seasoned salt; spread on steaks. Roll up as for jelly roll. Fasten with skewers and tie with string. Insert spit rod through center of meat rolls. Adjust holding forks; test balance. Place *medium* coals on both sides of drip pan. Attach spit; position drip pan under meat. Turn on motor. Grill over *medium* coals till done, about 45 minutes. Let stand a few minutes; remove strings and skewers.

In small saucepan heat sour cream over low heat; *do not boil*. Carefully carve meat rolls into thin slices and place on bread. Spoon warm sour cream atop meat. Serves 6.

PIZZA-FRANK SANDWICHES

1 beaten egg
¼ cup milk
¾ cup soft bread crumbs
¼ cup grated Parmesan cheese
2 tablespoons snipped parsley
½ teaspoon garlic salt
  Dash pepper
½ pound bulk pizza sausage
½ pound ground beef
6 frankfurters
1 8-ounce can pizza sauce
2 tablespoons chopped onion
2 tablespoons sliced pimento-
    stuffed green olives
6 frankfurter buns, split and
    toasted
⅓ cup shredded mozzarella cheese

Combine egg and milk; stir in crumbs, Parmesan cheese, parsley, garlic salt, and pepper. Add sausage and beef; mix thoroughly. Divide into 6 equal portions. Shape meat around frankfurters, leaving ends open; roll each between waxed paper to make uniform thickness. Chill.

In saucepan combine pizza sauce, chopped onion, and green olives. Simmer, uncovered, 5 minutes; stir occasionally. Grill frankfurters over *medium* coals till meat is set, about 5 minutes. Turn and grill till meat is done, about 10 minutes more. Brush with pizza sauce mixture during the last five minutes. Serve on toasted buns. Spoon remaining pizza sauce atop sandwiches and sprinkle with shredded mozzarella cheese. Makes 6 servings.

SPICED HAM PATTIES

1 slightly beaten egg
¼ cup milk
1½ cups soft bread crumbs (2 slices
     bread)
1 tablespoon finely chopped
     green onion with tops
   Dash pepper
1 pound ground cooked ham (3
     cups)
⅓ cup packed brown sugar
¼ cup honey
1 teaspoon dry mustard
¼ cup reserved spiced apple syrup
4 spiced apple rings

Combine the egg and milk; stir in bread crumbs, onion, and pepper. Add ham; mix well. Shape mixture into four 4-inch patties. In saucepan combine brown sugar, honey, dry mustard, and the spiced apple syrup; heat through. Grill patties over *medium-hot* coals for 5 minutes. Turn; brush with glaze. Place an apple ring atop each patty; brush with glaze. Grill ham patties till done, 5 to 6 minutes more. Pass remaining glaze with patties. Serves 4.

CORNED BEEF-TURKEY HEROES

8 Kaiser rolls *or* or hamburger
     buns, split
   Tartar sauce
   Russian, Italian, *or* blue cheese
     salad dressing
2 3- or 4-ounce packages thinly
     sliced smoked corned beef
8 thin onion slices
4 slices Swiss cheese, cut in half
2 3- or 4-ounce packages thinly
     sliced smoked turkey

Lightly spread cut surfaces of Kaiser rolls or buns with tartar sauce and salad dressing. Layer slices of the corned beef, onion, Swiss cheese, and turkey on rolls. Replace tops of rolls; place each sandwich on an 18x12-inch rectangle of heavy-duty foil. Wrap foil around sandwiches, sealing edges well. Grill over *medium* coals till heated through, about 25 minutes, turning several times. Serves 8.

BRATWURSTS IN BEER

1 12-ounce can beer (1½ cups)
2 tablespoons brown sugar
2 tablespoons soy sauce
1 tablespoon prepared mustard
1 teaspoon chili powder
2 cloves garlic, minced
  Several drops hot pepper sauce
6 bratwursts
6 individual French rolls
  Zesty Sauerkraut Relish (see
    recipe, page 116)

Combine beer, brown sugar, soy sauce, mustard, chili powder, garlic, and hot pepper sauce. Place brats in shallow baking dish; pour marinade over. Cover; refrigerate several hours or overnight, spooning marinade over occasionally. Remove brats, reserving marinade. Grill over *medium-hot* coals about 4 minutes. Turn and grill till done, 3 to 4 minutes more. Brush often with reserved marinade. Cut rolls in half lengthwise; hollow out rolls, leaving a ¼-inch wall. Fill each roll bottom with about ¼ cup drained relish. Add bratwurst and top with roll top. (Refrigerate remaining relish until needed.) Makes 6 servings.

ORIENTAL PORK WRAP-UPS

3 tablespoons chopped green onion
    with tops
4 teaspoons soy sauce
⅛ teaspoon garlic powder
1 pound ground pork
    Sweet-Sour Sauce
8 leaf lettuce leaves *or* lettuce cups
    Parsley Rice

Combine green onion, soy sauce, and garlic powder. Add ground pork; mix well. Shape mixture into eight 3x1-inch logs. Grill over *medium* coals for 4 to 5 minutes; turn and brush with Sweet-Sour Sauce. Grill logs till done, 3 to 4 minutes more. In center of each leaf lettuce place about 1 tablespoon Parsley Rice. Place a grilled log horizontally atop rice. Fold two opposite edges of lettuce crosswise so they overlap atop logs. Dip the bundle in Sweet-Sour Sauce for each bite. (Or, place rice in lettuce cups; top with pork log. Drizzle sauce over.) Serves 4.

Sweet-Sour Sauce: In saucepan combine ½ cup packed brown sugar and 1 tablespoon cornstarch. Stir in ⅓ cup red wine vinegar, ⅓ cup chicken broth, ¼ cup finely chopped green pepper, 2 tablespoons chopped pimento, 1 tablespoon soy sauce, ¼ teaspoon garlic powder, and ¼ teaspoon ground ginger. Place over *medium* coals, stirring occasionally, till thickened and bubbly. Makes 1¼ cups sauce.

Parsley Rice: In saucepan combine ⅔ cup water, ⅓ cup regular rice, and ¼ teaspoon salt. Cover with tight fitting lid. Bring to boiling over *medium* coals, about 15 minutes. Move to edge of coals; cook 10 minutes more (do not lift cover). Remove from heat; let stand, covered, 10 minutes. Stir in 2 tablespoons snipped parsley.

GRILLED CRAB AND CHEESE ROLLS

1 cup shredded Monterey Jack
     cheese (4 ounces)
¼ cup finely chopped celery
2 tablespoons mayonnaise *or* salad
     dressing
2 tablespoons chopped pimento
2 teaspoons lemon juice
1 teaspoon prepared mustard
1 7½-ounce can crab meat, drained,
     flaked, and cartilage removed
4 individual French rolls

Stir together cheese, celery, mayonnaise or salad dressing, pimento, lemon juice, and prepared mustard. Fold in crab. Split French rolls; spread crab mixture over bottom halves and replace tops. Wrap heavy-duty foil loosely around roll; fold edges of foil to seal tightly. Grill over *medium* coals for 10 minutes. Turn; grill till heated through, about 10 minutes more. Makes 4 servings.

Pork and Ham

APPLE-ORANGE STUFFED PORK CHOPS

    6 pork loin chops, cut 1½ inches
         thick
    ½ cup chopped celery
    ½ cup chopped unpeeled apple (1
         medium)
    2 tablespoons butter
    1 beaten egg
 1½ cups toasted raisin bread cubes
         (2½ slices)
    ½ teaspoon grated orange peel
    1 orange, sectioned and chopped
         (⅓ cup)
    ¼ teaspoon salt
    ⅛ teaspoon ground cinnamon

Make a slit in each chop by cutting from fat side almost to
bone. Season cavity with a little salt and pepper.

  In small saucepan cook celery and apple in butter till
tender but not brown. Combine egg, bread cubes, orange
peel, chopped orange, salt, and cinnamon. Pour cooked
celery and apple over bread cube mixture; toss lightly.
Spoon about ¼ cup stuffing into each pork chop. Securely
fasten pocket opening with wooden picks.

  Grill chops over *medium* coals about 20 minutes. Turn
meat and grill till done, 15 to 20 minutes more. Before
serving remove the picks. Makes 6 servings.

CORN-STUFFED PORK CHOPS

6 pork loin chops, cut 1½ inches
   thick
¼ cup chopped green pepper
¼ cup chopped onion
1 tablespoon butter *or* margarine
1 beaten egg
1½ cups toasted bread cubes
½ cup cooked whole kernel corn
2 tablespoons chopped pimento
½ teaspoon salt
¼ teaspoon ground cumin
   Dash pepper

Make a slit in each chop by cutting from fat side almost to
bone. Season cavity with a little salt and pepper.

In small saucepan cook green pepper and onion in butter till tender but not brown. Combine egg, bread cubes,
corn, pimento, salt, cumin, and pepper. Pour cooked pepper and onion over bread cube mixture; toss lightly. Spoon
about ¼ cup stuffing into each pork chop. Securely fasten
pocket opening with wooden picks.

Grill chops over *medium* coals about 20 minutes. Turn
meat and grill till done, 15 to 20 minutes more. Before
serving, remove the picks. Makes 6 servings.

ROAST PORK CHOPS

1 cup chopped onion
1 clove garlic, minced
2 tablespoons cooking oil
¾ cup catsup
¼ cup lemon juice
3 tablespoons sugar
2 tablespoon Worcestershire sauce
1 tablespoon prepared mustard
1 teaspoon salt
¼ teaspoon bottled hot pepper sauce
  Salt
6 pork loin chops *or* rib chops, cut
    1¼ to 1½ inches thick

In saucepan cook onion and garlic in hot oil till tender but not brown. Stir in catsup, lemon juice, sugar, Worcestershire sauce, prepared mustard, 1 teaspoon salt, and bottled hot pepper sauce. Simmer, uncovered, 5 minutes, stirring once or twice. Sprinkle chops with salt.

Place chops in wire grill basket. Grill chops over *medium* coals about 25 minutes. Turn meat and grill about 20 minutes more, brushing with sauce occasionally. Serves 6.

GYPSY PORK STEAKS

2 whole pork tenderloins (1½
    pounds)
4 teaspoons paprika
1 teaspoon salt
⅛ teaspoon pepper

Cut tenderloin into six 3-inch pieces. Resting each piece on cut side, flatten with side of cleaver or meat mallet to ¾-inch thickness. Stir together paprika, salt, and pepper. Coat meat on both sides with seasoning mixture. Grill pork over *medium* coals about 10 minutes. Turn meat and grill till done, about 10 minutes more. Serves 6.

APPLE-PEANUT BUTTERED PORK STEAKS

½ cup apple butter
2 tablespoons peanut butter
¼ teaspoon finely shredded orange
    peel
2 tablespoons orange juice
4 pork blade steaks, cut ¾ inch thick

Blend apple butter into peanut butter; add orange peel
and juice. Season steaks with salt and pepper. Grill over
medium coals for about 15 minutes. Turn steaks; brush
with apple butter mixture. Grill till done, 15 to 20 minutes
more. Brush on remaining apple butter mixture. Serves 4.

    Note: If desired, use 1½-inch-thick steaks. Grill 25 min-
utes. Turn; grill till done, about 25 minutes. Serves 8.

MARINATED PORK LOIN ROAST

1 5-pound boneless pork loin roast,
    rolled and tied
¼ cup water
3 tablespoons Dijon-style mustard
2 tablespoons cooking oil
1 tablespoon soy sauce

Pierce pork loin in several places with long-tined fork;
place in shallow baking dish. Blend water, mustard, oil, and
soy; brush over meat. Cover; let stand at room temperature 1 hour. Drain meat; reserve sauce. Insert spit rod
through center of roast. Adjust holding forks; test balance.
insert meat thermometer near center of roast, not touching rod. Place *medium-hot* coals on both sides of drip pan.
Attach spit; position drip pan under meat. Turn on motor.
Grill till thermometer register 170° for well-done, 2 to 2½
hours.

    During last 30 to 45 minutes, brush meat with mustard
sauce. Heat remaining sauce; pass with meat. Serves 8.

COMPANY PORK LOIN ROAST

1 cup catsup
¼ cup cooking oil
¼ cup wine vinegar
2 tablespoons instant minced onion
2 tablespoons Worcestershire sauce
1 tablespoon brown sugar
1 teaspoon mustard seed
1 teaspoon dried oregano, crushed
1 bay leaf
½ teaspoon salt
½ teaspoon cracked pepper
¼ teaspoon chili powder
1 t-pound boneless pork loin roast,
     rolled and tied

In saucepan, combine catsup, cooking oil, wine vinegar,
onion, Worcestershire sauce, brown sugar, mustard seed,
oregano, bay leaf, salt, pepper, chili powder, and ½ cup
water. Simmer the mixture 20 minutes; remove bay leaf.

Insert spit rod through center of roast. Adjust holding
forks and test balance. Insert meat thermometer near center of roast, not touching spit rod. In covered grill place
medium-hot coals on both sides of drip pan. Attach spit;
position drip pan under meat. Turn on motor; lower grill
hood or cover with foil tent. Grill till meat thermometer
registers 170° for well-done, 2 to 2½ hours. Brush with
sauce frequently during last 30 minutes. Serves 8.

HICKORY-SMOKED ROYAL RIBS

Hickory chips
¾ cup catsup
½ cup finely chopped onion
¼ cup olive oil *or* cooking oil
¼ cup tarragon vinegar
¼ cup water
3 tablespoons lemon juice
2 tablespoons Worcestershire sauce
1 tablespoon brown sugar
2 teaspoons dry mustard
2 teaspoons paprika
2 teaspoons chili powder
2 cloves garlic, minced
2 bay leaves
1 teaspoon cumin seed, crushed
1 teaspoon dried thyme, crushed
½ teaspoon salt
¼ teaspoon pepper
4 pounds pork loin back ribs *or*
   spareribs

Soak hickory chips in enough water to cover for about 1 hour before cooking time; drain. In saucepan stir together catsup, onion, oil, vinegar, water, lemon juice, Worcestershire sauce, brown sugar, dry mustard, paprika, chili powder, garlic, bay leaves, cumin seed, thyme, salt, and pepper; simmer 10 minutes.

Lace ribs accordion-style on spit; secure with holding forks. In covered grill place *hot* coals on both sides of foil drip pan. Sprinkle coals with some dampened hickory chips. Attach spit; position drip pan under meat. Turn on motor; lower the grill hood or cover with foil tent. Grill the ribs over hot coals till done, about 1 hour. Sprinkle the coals with chips every 20 minutes. Brush ribs frequently with sauce mixture during the last 15 minutes of cooking. Pass the remaining sauce. Serves 4 to 6.

LUAU SPARERIBS

1 cup pineapple preserves
2 tablespoons vinegar
2 tablespoons chopped pimento
1 tablespoon lemon juice
2 teaspoons Dijon-style mustard
1 teaspoon Kitchen Bouquet
3 to 4 pounds pork spareribs
   Salt
1 fresh pineapple, peeled and cut
     into lengthwise wedges
1 green pepper, cut into lengthwise strips

In a bowl combine the pineapple preserves, vinegar, pimento, lemon juice, mustard, and Kitchen Bouquet; set aside.

Sprinkle the ribs with salt. Lace ribs, pineapple wedges, and green pepper strips accordion-style on spit; secure with holding forks. In covered grill place *slow* coals on both sides of foil drip pan. Attach spit; position drip pan under meat. Turn on motor; lower grill hood or cover with foil tent.

Grill the ribs over *slow* coals till done, about 1 hour. During the last 15 minutes of cooking time, brush the meat, pineapple wedges, and green pepper occasionally with the pineapple glaze. Makes 3 or 4 servings.

For smoke flavor sprinkle coals with dampened hickory chips during the last 30 minutes of cooking.

How to
Barbecue Ribs

If your grill has a spit attachment, try using it to barbecue long strips of pork spareribs or pork loin back ribs. Simply lace the ribs on the spit accordion-style. Secure the ribs with holding forks so they'll stay in position while rotating over the coals.

CHINESE SMOKED RIBS

6 pounds pork loin back ribs *or*
    spareribs
2 tablespoons sugar
1 teaspoon salt
½ teaspoon paprika
½ teaspoon ground turmeric
¾ teaspoon celery seed
⅛ teaspoon dry mustard
    Hickory chips
½ cup catsup
½ cup packed brown sugar
1 tablespoon grated fresh
    gingerroot *or* 2 teaspoons
    ground ginger
1 clove garlic, minced

Thoroughly rub the ribs with mixture of sugar, salt, paprika, turmeric, celery seed, and dry mustard; cover and let stand 2 hours. About an hour before cooking time soak hickory chips in enough water to cover; drain.

In covered grill place *slow* coals on both sides of drip pan. Sprinkle coals with dampened hickory chips. Place ribs, bone side down, on grill; lower grill hood. Grill ribs over *slow* coals about 30 minutes. Turn meat and grill about 30 minutes more. Sprinkle coals with chips every 20 minutes. (If the thin end of spareribs cooks too quickly, place foil under thin end of ribs and continue cooking.)

Meanwhile, in saucepan combine catsup, brown sugar, soy sauce, ginger, and garlic. Cook and stir till sugar is dissolved. Brush mixture on both sides of ribs and grill, uncovered, till done, 10 to 15 minutes more. Heat any remaining sauce and serve with ribs. Makes 6 servings.

COUNTRY-STYLE BARBECUED RIBS

4 pounds pork country-style ribs
1 cup chopped onion
1 clove garlic, minced
¼ cup cooking oil
1 8-ounce can tomato sauce
½ cup water
¼ cup packed brown sugar
¼ cup lemon juice
2 tablespoons Worcestershire sauce
2 tablespoons prepared mustard
1 teaspoon salt
1 teaspoon celery seed
¼ teaspoon pepper

In large saucepan or Dutch oven cook ribs, covered, in enough boiling salted water to cover till ribs are tender, 45 to 60 minutes; drain well.

Meanwhile, in saucepan cook onion and garlic in hot oil till tender but not brown. Stir in tomato sauce, water, brown sugar, lemon juice, Worcestershire sauce, mustard, salt, celery seed, and pepper. Simmer, uncovered, 15 minutes; stir once or twice.

Grill ribs over *slow* coals till done, about 45 minutes, turning every 15 minutes. Brush with sauce till ribs are well coated. Makes 6 servings.

APRICOT GLAZED RIBS

4 pounds pork loin back ribs, cut
      in serving-size pieces
1½ cup water
1 cup snipped dried apricots
½ cup packed brown sugar
2 tablespoons vinegar
1 tablespoon lemon juice
1 teaspoon ground ginger
½ teaspoon salt

In large saucepan or Dutch oven cook ribs, covered, in enough boiling salted water to cover till ribs are tender, 45 to 60 minutes. Drain well; season the ribs with a little salt and pepper.

Meanwhile, in a small saucepan combine the 1½ cups water, apricots, brown sugar, vinegar, lemon juice, ginger, and salt. Bring the mixture to boiling. Reduce heat; cover and simmer 5 minutes. Pour mixture into blender container. Cover and blend till smooth.

Brush the glaze over the ribs. Grill ribs over *medium-slow* coals for 10 to 15 minutes. Turn ribs and grill till done, 10 to 15 minutes more; brush occasionally with the apricot glaze. Makes 4 servings.

GLAZED PORK KABOBS

    4 large carrots
    ½ cup apricot preserves
    ½ of an 8-ounce can tomato sauce
    ¼ cup packed brown sugar
    ¼ cup dry red wine
    2 tablespoons lemon juice
    2 tablespoons cooking oil
    1 teaspoon onion juice
 1½ pounds lean boneless pork
      Fresh pineapple chunks

Cut carrots into 1-inch pieces. In small saucepan cook, covered, in small amount boiling salted water for 15 to 20 minutes; drain. In saucepan combine apricot preserves, tomato sauce, brown sugar, wine, lemon juice, oil, and onion juice. Cook, uncovered, 10 to 15 minutes; stir occasionally. Cut pork into 1-inch cubes.

Thread pork, carrots, and pineapple chunks on six skewers; season with salt and pepper. Grill over *medium* coals about 10 minutes; turn frequently. Brush with sauce; grill till done, about 5 minutes more. Makes 6 servings.

KOREAN KABOBS

1½ pounds lean boneless pork
 ½ cup unsweetened pineapple
     juice
 ¼ cup soy sauce
 ¼ cup sliced green onion with tops
 4 teaspoons sesame seed
 1 tablespoon brown sugar
 1 clove garlic, minced
 ⅛ teaspoon pepper
 1 teaspoon cornstarch
 1 green pepper

Cut pork into 18 pieces. In large bowl combine pineapple juice, soy sauce, green onion, sesame seed, brown sugar, garlic, and pepper; add meat pieces. Cover; refrigerate overnight or let stand 2 hours at room temperature, turning meat occasionally in the marinade.

Drain meat; reserve marinade. In saucepan blend cornstarch and 2 tablespoons water; stir in reserved marinade. Cook and stir till thickened. Cut green pepper into 1-inch squares. Thread pepper on six skewers alternately with meat. Grill over *medium* coals 6 to 8 minutes. Turn kabobs; grill till done, 6 to 8 minutes more, brushing with sauce occasionally. Pass remaining sauce. Serves 6.

How to Spit-Roast a Pig

Obtain a small dressed pig. (Plan on 60 to 70 servings from a 60-pound dressed pig—live weight, 90 to 100 pounds.)

Rent a large barbecue or follow these general guidelines for making a barbecue pit. In a grassless place, dig a pit 12 inches deep and as wide and long as the pig. Arrange charcoal in two lengthwise rows, 12 to 15 inches apart. Drive notched pipes into ground to hold spit about 16 inches above coals. Rig up motor-driven rotisserie. (Or plan to turn spitted pig by hand throughout roasting period.)

Insert spit rod through center cavity of dressed pig; test balance. Secure pig well with wires and/or wire mesh. Tie legs together; cover tail and ears with foil. Place drip pan between rows of *hot* coals. Balance spit on pipes. Position drip pan under pig. Start motor or begin turning.

Pig will shrink as it roasts; have tools handy to tighten wires. Use a water-filled sprinkler to put out any flare-ups. (Fires are more frequent during the first or second hour.) Do not baste pig. Add *hot* coals to maintain constant heat.

Allow about 8 hours for 60-pound pig to be done. Time varies with heat of coals and size of pig. Check doneness by placing meat thermometer in center of thigh of hind leg; make sure it doesn't touch bone or spit rod. Roast till meat thermometer registers 170° to 185°. Have large, clean surface available for carving. Generally, meat will be so thoroughly cooked that it will fall off the bones.

ORANGE-GINGER HAM GRILL

¼ cup frozen orange juice
   concentrate, thawed
¼ cup dry white wine
1 teaspoon dry mustard
¼ teaspoon ground ginger
1 1½-to 2-pound fully cooked ham
   slice, cut 1 inch thick
6 canned pineapple slices
   Orange slices (optional)

Combine orange juice concentrate, wine, mustard, and
ginger. Slash fat edge of ham slice. Brush sauce over ham.
Grill over *medium* coals for 10 to 15 minutes, brushing
with sauce occasionally. Turn ham and grill till done, 10 to
15 minutes more, brushing with sauce. Grill pineapple
slices alongside the ham, brushing frequently with sauce.
Place pineapple atop ham during last 5 to 10 minutes of
grilling. Garnish with orange slices, if desired. Makes 6
servings.

HAM SLICE WITH CRANBERRY SAUCE

1 8-ounce can jellied cranberry
   sauce
2 tablespoons bottled steak sauce
1 tablespoon cooking oil
2 teaspoons brown sugar
1 teaspoon prepared mustard
1 1½-pound fully cooked ham slice,
   cut 1 inch thick

Combine jellied cranberry sauce, steak sauce, cooking oil,
brown sugar, and prepared mustard. Beat with electric
mixer or rotary beater till smooth.

Slash fat edge of ham slice. Grill over *medium* coals for 10 to 15 minutes, brushing with sauce occasionally. Turn ham and grill till done, 10 to 15 minutes more, brushing with sauce. Heat remaining sauce on edge of grill; serve with ham. Makes 4 or 5 servings.

FRUIT-GLAZED HAM

Apricot Glaze or Grape Glaze
1 1½-pound fully cooked center cut
   ham slice, cut 1 inch thick

Prepare one of the fruit glazes. Slash fat edge of ham slice to prevent curling. Place ham slice in shallow dish; pour glaze mixture over ham. Cover; refrigerate overnight or let stand at room temperature for 2 hours, spooning glaze over ham several times. Remove ham, reserving glaze.

Grill ham slice over *medium* coals for 10 to 15 minutes, brushing with glaze occasionally. Turn ham and grill till done, 10 to 15 minutes more, brushing with glaze. Heat the remaining glaze in small saucepan on edge of grill. To serve cut the ham into slices and pass heated fruit glaze. Makes 6 servings.

Apricot Glaze: In saucepan combine ½ cup apricot preserves, 2 tablespoons prepared mustard, 1 tablespoon water, 2 teaspoons lemon juice, 1 teaspoon Worcestershire sauce, and ⅛ teaspoon ground cinnamon. Heat, stirring occasionally, till preserves melt.

Grape Glaze: In saucepan combine ½ cup grape jelly, 2 tablespoons prepared mustard, 1½ teaspoons lemon juice, and ⅛ teaspoon ground cinnamon. Heat, stirring occasionally, till jelly melts.

ORANGE-SAUCED HAM

1 5-pound boneless fully cooked
    canned ham
1 10-ounce jar currant jelly
¾ cup light corn syrup
2 tablespoons cornstarch
1 teaspoon grated orange peel
½ cup orange juice
¾ teaspoon ground nutmeg
  Orange slices
  Parsley sprigs

Insert spit rod through center of ham. Adjust holding forks; test balance. Insert meat thermometer near center of ham, not touching rod. In covered grill place *medium* coals on both sides of drip pan. Attach spit; position drip pan under ham. Turn on motor; lower grill hood or cover with foil tent. Grill ham over *medium* coals till done and meat thermometer registers 140°, 1 to 1¼ hours. (If grill does not have spit, see Note.) Meanwhile, in saucepan combine jelly, corn syrup, cornstarch, orange peel and juice, and nutmeg. Cook, stirring constantly, till sauce is thickened. Brush over ham frequently during last 15 minutes of cooking. Heat remaining sauce; pass with ham. Garnish ham with orange slices and parsley. Serves 12.

Note: If grill does not have spit, place ham directly on grill over drip pan. Lower hood or tent grill with heavy-duty foil. Grill ham over *medium* coals for 1 hour. Lift foil tent; turn ham. Insert meat thermometer and brush with sauce. Recover grill with foil tent. Roast ham till thermometer registers 140°, about 30 minutes more.

SWEET-SOUR HAM

1 5-pound boneless fully cooked
    canned ham
1 20-ounce can pineapple slices
¼ cup dry sherry *or* dry white
    wine
3 tablespoons vinegar
2 tablespoons soy sauce
2 tablespoons honey
1 tablespoon cooking oil
1 clove garlic, minced
    Dash salt
2 small green peppers, cut in 1½-
    inch squares
12 cherry tomatoes
2 limes, cut in wedges

Insert spit rod through center of ham. Adjust holding
forks; test balance. Insert meat thermometer near center
of ham, not touching rod. In covered grill place *medium*
coals on both sides of drip pan. Attach spit; position drip
pan under meat. Turn on motor; lower grill hood or cover
with foil tent. Grill ham over *medium* coals till done and
meat thermometer registers 140°, 1 to 1¼ hours. (If grill
does not have spit, see Note above.) Meanwhile, drain
pineapple, reserving ⅓ cup syrup. Set drained pineapple
aside. In saucepan combine the reserved syrup, dry sherry,
vinegar, soy, honey, cooking oil, garlic, and salt. Boil mixture down to equal ⅔ cup (about 10 minutes); stir occasionally. During last 30 minutes of cooking, brush ham
often with sauce; pass remaining sauce. Before serving,
quarter each pineapple slice. Thread 12 small bamboo
skewers with green pepper, pieces of pineapple, cherry
tomato, and lime wedge. Serve with ham. Serves 12.

SKEWERED HAM AND FRUIT KABOBS

1 8-ounce can pineapple slices
½ cup extra-hot catsup
½ cup orange marmalade
2 tablespoons finely chopped onion
1 tablespoon cooking oil
1 to 1½ teaspoons dry mustard
2 pounds fully cooked boneless
    ham, cut into 1-inch cubes
2 oranges, cut in wedges
1 16-ounce jar spiced crab apples

Drain pineapple slices, reserving ⅓ cup syrup. Quarter each pineapple slice and set aside. In saucepan stir together the pineapple syrup, catsup, orange marmalade, onion, oil, and dry mustard. Simmer, uncovered, for about 5 minutes, stirring once or twice.

On six skewers thread ham cubes and orange wedges. Grill over *medium* coals about 15 minutes, turning frequently and brushing with sauce. Thread crab apples and pineapple pieces on ends of skewers. Grill till meat and fruits are hot, 5 to 10 minutes longer, turning the kabobs often and brushing with the sauce. Makes 6 servings.

PINEAPPLE-GLAZED LUNCHEON MEAT

⅔ cup pineapple preserves
⅓ cup packed brown sugar
¼ cup lemon juice
¼ cup prepared mustard
    Whole cloves
3 12-ounce cans luncheon meat

Combine preserves, brown sugar, lemon juice, and mustard. Score each piece of meat in diamonds, cutting only ¼ inch deep. (A strip of heavy paper makes an easy guide for cutting parallel lines.) Stud meat with cloves. Insert spit rod lengthwise through center of each luncheon meat. Secure with holding forks; test balance. In covered grill arrange *hot* coals on both sides of drip pan. Attach spit; position drip pan under meat. Turn on motor; lower grill hood or cover with foil tent. Grill meat over *hot* coals till done, 35 to 40 minutes. During last 10 minutes baste meat often with sauce. Pass remaining sauce. Serves 10 to 12.

MEAT AND POTATO BAKE

4 large baking potatoes
  Cooking oil
1 12-ounce can luncheon meat
4 slices American cheese, cut in
    half diagonally (3 ounces)
  Grated Parmesan cheese
  Butter *or* margarine

Rub potatoes with oil. Wrap each potato in 18 x 12-inch rectangle of heavy-duty foil; seal edges well. Grill over *medium* coals for 1½ hours; turn frequently. (Or, cook on covered grill over *medium-slow* coals for 1½ to 2 hours.)

Remove from grill; unwrap. Slice each potato crosswise into four pieces. Cut meat in half crosswise; cut each half into six slices crosswise. Insert slices of meat between potato pieces. Reassemble potato; rewrap in foil, closing top. (Or, skewer potato together and omit foil.)

Grill till heated through, 10 to 15 minutes more; turn twice. Remove foil; place 2 cheese triangles atop each potato. Sprinkle with Parmesan; serve with butter. Serves 4.

VEGETABLE-MEAT KABOBS

3 medium yams *or* sweet potatoes
1 9-ounce package frozen Brussels
      sprouts
1 12-ounce can luncheon meat
½ cup cooking oil
¼ cup vinegar
½ teaspoon celery seed
1 envelope French salad dressing mix
4 to 8 cherry tomatoes

Cook yams, covered, in enough boiling salted water to cover for 25 to 30 minutes, drain. Cool; peel and cut into 1-inch chunks. Cook sprouts in boiling salted water 5 minutes; drain. Cut meat in 1-inch cubes. In bowl mix oil, vinegar, celery seed, dressing mix, and dash pepper; blend well. Stir in meat and sprouts. Cover; refrigerate 4 to 6 hours, stirring often. Drain; reserve marinade. Thread meat, Brussels sprouts, and yams on four skewers. Grill over *hot* coals for 5 minutes. Turn; add tomatoes to skewers. Grill till meat is heated through, about 5 minutes more. Baste often with reserved marinade. Serves 4.

SUPER-SIMPLE SKILLET SUPPER

1 12-ounce can luncheon meat
1   16-ounce can cut green beans
1½ cups water
1 5½-ounce package dry hash
      brown potatoes with onion.
1 5½-ounce can evaporated milk
1 5-ounce jar cheese spread with
      hickory smoke flavor

Cut luncheon meat into strips. In skillet combine luncheon meat, undrained green beans, water, dry potatoes, milk, cheese spread, and dash pepper. Cover; cook over *medium* coals, stirring occasionally. Heat till mixture is bubbly and potatoes are tender, about 10 minutes. Serves 4.

Poultry

HICKORY-SMOKED TURKEY

Hickory chips
1 12-pound turkey
1 tablespoon salt
¼ cup cooking oil

Soak hickory chips in enough water to cover, about an hour before cooking. Drain chips. Rinse bird and pat dry; rub cavity with salt. Skewer neck skin to back. Tuck wing tips behind shoulder joints. Push drumsticks under band of skin or tie to tail.

In covered grill arrange *medium-slow* coals around edge of grill. Sprinkle coals with some of dampened chips. Center foil pan on grill, not directly over coals. Place bird, breast side up, in foil pan; brush with oil. Insert meat thermometer in center of inside thigh muscle without touching bone. Lower grill hood. Grill over *medium-slow* coals till thermometer registers 185°, 3½ to 4½ hours. Sprinkle hickory chips over coals every 20 to 30 minutes. Brush bird often with additional oil. Add more coals, if needed. Let the turkey stand 15 minutes before carving. Makes 12 servings.

BARBECUED LEMON TURKEY

1 6-to 7-pound turkey
¼ cup cooking oil
¼ cup soy sauce
¼ cup finely chopped onion
1 teaspoon sugar
1 teaspoon ground turmeric
1 teaspoon ground ginger
½ teaspoon grated lemon peel
2 tablespoons lemon juice

Have meatman cut frozen turkey in half lengthwise. At home thaw turkey. Cut into pieces: 2 wings, 2 drumsticks, 2 thighs, 4 breast pieces, and 2 back pieces.

In large plastic bag combine oil, soy sauce, onion, sugar, turmeric, ginger, lemon peel, and juice. Place turkey pieces in bag; close bag.

Marinate turkey in the refrigerator 6 hours or overnight. Drain, reserving marinade. In covered grill place thighs and breast pieces over *slow* coals. Lower hood and grill about 30 minutes, turning pieces occasionally. Add drumsticks, wings, and back pieces. Lower hood; grill about 1 hour more, turning pieces occasionally. During the last 15 minutes, brush turkey pieces with the reserved marinade. Serves 6 to 8.

SMOKED TURKEY ROAST

Hickory chips
1 3½- to 4-pound frozen boneless
    turkey roast, thawed
¼ cup cooking oil
1 tablespoon snipped parsley
2 teaspoons dried sage, crushed
¼ teaspoon lemon pepper marinade

Soak the hickory chips in enough water to cover, about an hour before cooking. Drain chips. Insert spit rod through center of turkey roast. Adjust holding forks; test balance. Insert meat thermometer in center of roast, not touching metal rod. In covered grill place *slow* coals on both sides of drip pan. Attach spit; position drip pan directly under roast. Turn on motor. Place a small pan of water at one end of firebox for moisture. Sprinkle coals with some dampened chips; lower grill hood or cover with foil tent. Grill roast over *slow* coals till thermometer registers 185°, 2½ to 3 hours. Brush roast occasionally with mixture of oil, parsley, sage, and lemon pepper. Sprinkle chips over coals every 20 minutes. Let roast stand 10 minutes before carving. Serves 8 to 10.

ROTISSERIE-ROAST TURKEY

6 tablespoons butter *or* margarine,
    melted
¼ cup dry white wine
1 clove garlic, minced
½ teaspoon dried rosemary, crushed
1 5-to 6-pound frozen boneless
    turkey roast, thawed
  Salt
  Pepper

Combine *4 tablespoons* of the butter, the wine, garlic, and rosemary. Keep at room temperature to blend flavors.

Insert spit rod through center of turkey roast. Adjust holding forks; test balance. Insert meat thermometer in center of roast, not touching metal rod. Brush roast with remaining 2 tablespoons butter; season with salt and pepper. Place *hot* coals on both sides of foil drip pan. Attach spit; position drip pan directly under roast. Turn on motor. Grill turkey over *hot* coals till thermometer registers 185°, 2½ to 3 hours. During the last 30 minutes, baste roast with wine sauce. Makes 16 to 18 servings.

SWEET-SOUR CORNISH HENS

4 1-to 1½-pound Cornish game
      hens
   Salt
   Pepper
¼ cup butter *or* margarine, melted
1 10-ounce jar sweet and sour
      sauce
1 8-ounce can tomatoes, cut up
1 teaspoon soy sauce
6 thin slices lemon, halved

Season cavity of each hen with a little salt and pepper. Skewer neck and tail openings closed. Run spit rod through each hen crosswise, below breastbone. With four 18-inch cords, use one cord to tie each tail to crossed legs. Bring cord around to back, cross and bring around and across breast securing wings to body. Tie knot, cut off loose ends. Space birds about 1 inch apart on rod; secure with holding forks. Test balance. Place *hot* coals on both sides of drip pan. Attach spit; position drip pan under hens. Turn on motor. Grill hens till leg joints move easily, about 45 minutes. Baste hens often with melted butter.

Meanwhile, in saucepan combine sweet and sour sauce, tomatoes, soy sauce, and lemon slices; heat just to boiling. Grill hens about 15 minutes more, basting often with sauce. Pass extra sauce. Makes 4 servings.

CORNISH HENS WITH RICE STUFFING

1   6-ounce package long grain and
    wild rice mix
¼   cup light raisins
2   tablespoons butter *or* margarine
2   tablespoons blanched slivered
    almonds
½   teaspoon ground sage
    Salt
4   1- to 1½-pound Cornish game
    hens
¼   cup butter *or* margarine, melted

Cook rice mix according to package directions; stir in raisins, 2 tablespoons butter, almonds, and sage. Rub cavities of each hen with salt. Skewer neck skin to back. Fill each body cavity with about ¾ cup rice stuffing; cover opening with foil. Tie legs to tail; twist wing tips under back. Brush hens with ¼ cup melted butter. Arrange *medium-hot* coals around edge of grill. Center foil pan on grill, not directly over coals. Place birds in foil pan, allowing space between each bird. Grill hens over medium-hot coals till tender, 1½ to 1¾ hours. Brush occasionally with the drippings on foil. Serves 4.

KOWLOON DUCKLING

Hickory chips
1   4-to 5-pound duckling
6 to 8 green onions with tops, cut
    up
6 sprigs parsley
1 clove garlic, minced
½ cup soy sauce
2 tablespoons honey
2 tablespoons lemon juice
    Plum Sauce

Soak the hickory chips in enough water to cover, about an hour before cooking. Drain chips. Stuff cavity of duckling with onion, parsley, and garlic. Skewer neck and body cavities closed; tie legs to tail securely with cord. In saucepan heat soy sauce, honey, and lemon juice. In covered grill arrange *slow* coals around edge of grill. Sprinkle coals with some of the dampened chips. Center foil pan on grill, not directly over coals. Place duck, breast up, in foil pan. Lower grill hood. Grill for 2¼ to 2½ hours. Sprinkle chips over coals every 30 minutes. Brush duck often with soy mixture. Remove drippings from pan as needed. Serve with Plum Sauce. Serves 2 or 3.

Plum Sauce: Drain one 16-ounce can purple plums, reserving ¼ cup syrup. Force plums through a sieve. In saucepan combine the sieved plums, plum syrup, ¼ teaspoon grated orange peel, 3 tablespoons orange juice, 2 tablespoons sugar, ½ teaspoon Worcestershire sauce, and ¼ teaspoon ground cinnamon. Heat the mixture to boiling; reduce heat and simmer 10 minutes.

GRILLED ISLAND CHICKEN

- 1   8¼-ounce can crushed pineapple
- ¾   cup packed brown sugar
- 3   tablespoons lemon juice
- 1   tablespoon prepared mustard
- 2   2½-to 3-pound ready-to-cook
    broiler-fryer chickens, split in
    half lengthwise
- ½   cup cooking oil
- 1½ teaspoons salt
- ¼   teaspoon pepper

Drain pineapple and reserve 2 tablespoons syrup.
Combine pineapple, reserved syrup, sugar, lemon juice,
and mustard. Break wing, hip, and drumstick joints of
chickens; twist wing tips under back. Brush chickens well
with oil; season with salt and ¼ teaspoon pepper. Grill
chickens over *slow* coals, bone side down, till bone side is
well browned, 20 to 30 minutes. Turn chicken; grill till tender, about 30 minutes more. Turn and brush chickens
often with glaze last 10 minutes. Serves 4.

CORN-STUFFED CHICKEN BREASTS

8 whole chicken breasts
¼ cup chopped onion
¼ cup chopped celery
2 tablespoons butter
1 8¾-ounce can whole kernel corn,
    drained (1 cup)
1 cup herb-seasoned stuffing mix
1 slightly beaten egg
½ teaspoon poultry seasoning
¼ teaspoon salt
¼ cup butter, melted

Cut breasts through white cartilage at V of neck. Using both hands, grasp the small bones on either side. Bend each side back, pushing up with fingers to snap out breastbone, keeping meat in one piece. Do *not* remove skin. Sprinkle cut side with salt. In skillet cook onion and celery in the 2 tablespoons butter till tender. Add corn, stuffing mix, egg, poultry seasoning, and salt; mix well. Spoon some corn mixture on cut side of each chicken breast. Fold over and skewer or tie closed. Grill chicken over *medium-hot* coals till tender, 30 to 35 minutes, turning often. Brush with the ¼ cup melted butter during the last 10 minutes. Serves 8.

CHICKEN TERIYAKI

½ cup packed brown sugar
½ cup soy sauce
2 tablespoons sweet sake, mirin, *or*
    dry sherry
1 tablespoon grated onion
1 clove garlic, minced
4 whole large chicken breasts, split,
    skinned, and boned
  Nonstick vegetable spray coating
    or cooking oil

In saucepan stir together brown sugar, soy, sake, onion, and garlic. Cook and stir over low heat till sugar dissolves. Cook, uncovered, till like thin syrup, about 5 minutes more; cool. Place chicken in shallow baking dish. Pour soy mixture over chicken. Cover; refrigerate 4 to 6 hours or overnight, occasionally spooning marinade over.

Remove chicken; reserve marinade. Coat grill with nonstick spray coating or cooking oil. Grill chicken over *medium-hot* coals for 15 to 20 minutes; turn often. Brush frequently with reserved marinade. Serves 8.

SAUSAGE-STUFFED CHICKEN ROLL-UPS

6 whole large chicken breasts,
    skinned and boned
2 tablespoons chopped green onion
    with tops
6 fully cooked smoked sausage
    links
½ cup butter, melted
¼ cup white wine *or* dry sherry
¼ cup snipped parsley
½ teaspoon paprika
    Cooking oil

Place chicken breasts one at a time between two sheets of waxed paper. Working out from center, pound to form 8 x 8-inch cutlets. Remove paper; sprinkle each cutlet with a little salt and *1 teaspoon* of the green onion. Place a sausage link at the end of each cutlet. Tuck in sides; roll up as for jelly roll. Press end to seal well; secure with wooden picks. Blend next four ingredients. Coat grill with cooking oil. Grill chicken, seam side down, over *medium-hot* coals about 15 minutes, turning often and brushing with butter mixture. Grill till done, 8 to 10 minutes more, turning and brushing with butter mixture. Serves 6.

CHICKEN WITH ZUCCHINI STUFFING

2   2½- to 3-pound whole ready-to-
    cook broiler-fryer chickens
1½ cups chicken broth
⅔   cup regular rice
2   cups chopped zucchini
1   cup shredded carrot
½   cup chopped onion
¾   teaspoon salt
⅛   teaspoon pepper
½   cup chicken broth
¼   cup grated Parmesan cheese
1½ teaspoons dried chervil, crushed
    Cooking oil

Sprinkle cavity of birds with salt. In saucepan combine 1½ cups chicken broth and rice. Bring to boiling; cover. Reduce heat; cook 14 minutes. *Do not drain.* In another saucepan combine zucchini, carrot, onion, salt, pepper, and remaining ½ cup broth. Cook, covered, just till tender, about 10 minutes. *Do not drain.* Stir in Parmesan cheese and chervil. Fold in rice. Spoon mixture loosely into bird cavities. Skewer neck skin to back of chickens. Mount one chicken on spit rod (see tip page 78). Repeat with second fork and chicken. Add a third holding fork, pressing tines into meat; test balance. Place *medium* coals around drip pan under meat. Turn on motor; lower hood or cover with foil tent. Brush birds with cooking oil. Grill over *medium* coals till done, about 2 hours. Serves 8.

HERB-GLAZED CHICKENS

2 2½- to 3-pound whole ready-to-
   cook broiler-fryer chickens
½ cup cooking oil
¼ cup light corn syrup
¼ cup finely chopped onion
1 tablespoon lemon juice
1 teaspoon dried oregano, crushed
1 teaspoon caraway seed
½ teaspoon salt

Salt chicken cavities. Skewer neck skin to back of chickens.
Mount one chicken on spit rod (see tip page 78). Repeat
with second fork and chicken. Add a third holding fork,
pressing tines into meat; test balance. Place *medium-hot*
coals around drip pan. Attach spit; position drip pan under
meat. Turn on motor; lower hood or cover with foil tent.
Grill chickens over *medium-hot* coals till tender, 1½ to 1¾
hours. Position drip pan under meat. Meanwhile, combine
remaining seven ingredients. Brush over chicken occasionally last 30 minutes. Serves 6 to 8.

---

*How to Mount Birds
for Spit Roasting*

Proper balance and correct timings are the keys to
success when spit-roasting. (A) Place one holding
fork on spit rod, tines toward point. Insert rod
through bird lengthwise. Pinch fork tines together;
push into breast. (B) Tie wings, using 24 inches of
cord. Start cord at back; loop around each wing.
Wrap around wings again. Tie in center of breast.
Loop an 18-inch cord around tail, then around
crossed legs; tie tightly to hold bird securely. (C) Pull
together cords attached to wings and legs; tie tightly.
Secure bird with second holding fork.

CURRY BARBECUED CHICKEN

2 2½- to 3-pound ready-to-cook
     broiler-fryer chickens
½ cup cooking oil
1 teaspoon grated lime peel
¼ cup lime juice
1 tablespoon grated onion
1 clove garlic, minced
2 teaspoons curry powder
½ teaspoon salt
½ teaspoon ground cumin
½ teaspoon ground coriander
¼ teaspoon ground cinnamon
¼ teaspoon pepper
    Lime slices
    Parsley

Quarter chickens. Break wing, hip, and drumstick joints of chickens so pieces will remain flat. Twist wing tips under back. Combine cooking oil, lime peel and juice, onion, garlic, curry powder, salt, cumin, coriander, cinnamon, and pepper. Place chickens in large plastic bag set in deep bowl. Pour marinade mixture over chickens. Close bag; refrigerate 4 to 6 hours, turning bag occasionally to coat chickens evenly.

Remove chickens, reserving marinade. Place chicken pieces, bone side down, over *medium-hot* coals. Grill chickens about 25 minutes. Turn, bone side up, and grill till done, 15 to 20 minutes more. Brush chickens with marinade frequently last 10 minutes. Garnish with lime twists and parsley. Makes 8 servings.

CHICKEN AND VEGETABLE BUNDLES

4 chicken drumsticks, skinned
4 chicken thighs, skinned
2 large potatoes, peeled and cubed
1 8-ounce can sliced carrots,
    drained
1 8-ounce can cut green beans,
    drained
1 small onion, sliced and separated
    into rings
4 tablespoons butter *or* margarine
½ teaspoon dried tarragon, crushed
½ teaspoon hickory-smoked salt

Tear off four 18 x 18-inch pieces of heavy-duty foil. On each piece of foil, place one chicken leg and one thigh; sprinkle chicken with salt and pepper. Top each serving with a *few pieces* of potato, carrots, green beans, and onion. Place 1 tablespoon butter in each bundle; sprinkle each with some of the tarragon and hickory-smoked salt. Bring 4 corners of foil to center, twist securely, allowing room for expansion of steam. Grill the chicken bundles over *slow* coals till chicken is tender, about 1 hour. Makes 4 servings.

SPICY BARBECUED CHICKEN

¼ cup finely chopped onion
1 clove garlic, minced
2 tablespoons cooking oil
¾ cup catsup
⅓ cup vinegar
1 teaspoon grated lemon peel
1 tablespoon lemon juice
1 tablespoon Worcestershire sauce
2 teaspoons sugar
1 teaspoon dry mustard
½ teaspoon pepper
¼ teaspoon bottled hot pepper sauce
2 2½- to 3-pound ready-to-cook
    broiler-fryer chickens

Cook onion and garlic in oil till tender but not brown. Stir in catsup, vinegar, lemon peel and juice, Worcestershire sauce, sugar, dry mustard, salt, pepper, and bottled hot pepper sauce. Simmer, covered, about 30 minutes; stir occasionally. Quarter chickens. Break wing, hip, and drumstick joints of chickens so pieces will remain flat. Twist wing tips under back. Season chicken pieces with additional salt and pepper.

Place chicken pieces, bone side down, over *medium-hot* coals. Grill chickens about 25 minutes. Turn, bone side up, and grill till done, 15 to 20 minutes more. Brush chickens with sauce often last 10 minutes. Makes 8 servings.

LEMONADE CHICKEN

2 2½- to 3-pound ready-to-cook
    broiler-fryer chickens
1 6-ounce can frozen lemonade
    concentrate, thawed
⅓ cup soy sauce
1 teaspoon seasoned salt
½ teaspoon celery salt
⅛ teaspoon garlic powder

Cut the chickens into serving pieces. In small bowl combine thawed lemonade concentrate, soy sauce, seasoned
salt, celery salt, and garlic powder. Stir mixture to blend
well. Dip chicken pieces in lemonade mixture. Place
chicken, bone side down, over *medium-hot* coals. Grill
about 25 minutes. Turn, bone side up, and grill till done,
15 to 20 minutes more. Brush chicken with lemonade mixture frequently last 10 minutes. Makes 8 servings.

JAPANESE-STYLE CHICKEN

4 whole large chicken breasts
¼ cup peanut oil *or* cooking oil
¼ cup soy sauce
¼ cup dry sherry
1 tablespoon brown sugar
1 tablespoon grated fresh
    gingerroot *or* 1 teaspoon
    ground ginger
1 clove garlic, minced
½ teaspoon salt
18 fresh mushroom caps
3 medium zucchini, cut in 1-inch
    slices (about 18 pieces)

Cut breasts through white cartilage at V of neck. Using
both hands, grasp the small bones on either side. Bend

each side back, pushing up with fingers to snap out breast-bone. To split breast, cut in two lengthwise pieces. Working out from center, pound each to form 5 x 5-inch cutlet. Cut into strips about 1 inch wide. Combine next seven ingredients. Place chicken in shallow baking dish; pour marinade over. Cover; refrigerate 4 to 6 hours, spooning marinade over occasionally. Remove chicken, reserving marinade. Pour some boiling water over mushrooms in bowl. Let stand 1 minute; drain. On long skewers thread chicken accordion-style alternately with zucchini and mushrooms. Grill over *medium-hot* coals for 12 to 15 minutes; turning and basting often with marinade. Serves 6.

CHICKEN AND BEEF KABOBS

    1 pound beef sirloin steak
    1 14½-ounce can pineapple slices
    ½ cup catsup
    3 tablespoons vinegar
    2 teaspoons instant beef bouillon
        granules
    ¼ cup finely chopped onion
    1 teaspoon celery seed
    ½ teaspoon ground cinnamon
    ¼ teaspoon ground allspice
    1 bay leaf
   12 small whole chicken wings

Cut beef in 1-inch pieces. Drain pineapple; reserve syrup. Cover and refrigerate pineapple. Add water to syrup, if necessary, to measure ¾ cup liquid; combine with catsup, vinegar, bouillon, onion, celery seed, cinnamon, allspice, and bay leaf. Add meat pieces to marinade. Cover; refrigerate several hours, stirring occasionally. Drain meat, reserving marinade. Quarter each pineapple slice; place 2 pieces together. Thread on skewers alternately with beef and chicken. Grill over *hot* coals till done, about 20 minutes, turning and brushing occasionally with reserved marinade. Heat remaining marinade; pass with kabobs. Makes 6 servings.

*Microwave Helps
to Shorten Grilling Time*

Yes, it is possible to get barbecue-flavored chicken in a hurry. The secret: precook chicken pieces in a countertop microwave oven before putting them on grill. For example, place a single layer of chicken pieces in a 10 x 6 x 2-inch baking dish and microcook, covered, about 15 minutes. Then grill over *medium-hot* coals till tender, 10 to 15 minutes more; turn chicken till evenly browned.

Fish and Seafood

WINE-SAUCED TROUT

1 15-ounce can tomato sauce
½ cup dry red wine
½ cup butter *or* margarine
2 tablespoons lemon juice
2 tablespoons chopped green onion
    with tops
1 teaspoon sugar
1 teaspoon dried salad herbs
½ teaspoon salt
    Few drops bottled hot pepper
    sauce
6 whole pan-dressed lake *or* brook
    trout *or* perch (about 8 ounces
    each)

In small saucepan combine tomato sauce, wine, butter, lemon juice, green onion, sugar, salad herbs, salt, and hot pepper sauce. Simmer, uncovered, 10 to 15 minutes. Grill fish over *hot* coals 10 to 12 minutes. Turn fish and grill till done, 10 to 12 minutes more. Brush fish with sauce during last few minutes of grilling. Pass the warm sauce. Makes 6 servings.

SKILLET-FRIED FISH

6 fresh *or* frozen pan-dressed trout
   or other fish (about 6 ounces
   each)
⅓ cup yellow cornmeal
¼ cup all-purpose flour
2 teaspoons salt
1 teaspoon dried parsley flakes
½ teaspoon paprika
1 5⅓-ounce can evaporated milk (⅔
   cup)
   Cooking oil

Thaw fish, if frozen. Thoroughly stir together cornmeal, flour, salt, dried parsley, and paprika. Dip fish in evaporated milk, then coat with seasoned cornmeal mixture.

Heat a small amount of cooking oil in a large skillet over *hot* coals till oil is hot. Cook fish, a few at a time, in hot oil till lightly browned, 4 to 5 minutes. Turn and cook till fish flakes easily with a fork, 4 to 5 minutes more. Add more oil as needed. Drain the fish on paper toweling before serving. Makes 6 servings.

HICKORY-SMOKED STUFFED TROUT

Hickory chips
¼ cup chopped onion
2 tablespoons butter *or* margarine
¼ cup snipped dried apricots
3 tablespoons orange juice
1 teaspoon sugar
1 teaspoon instant chicken bouillon
    granules
¼ teaspoon celery salt
2 cups dry bread cubes (2½ slices
    bread)
2 tablespoons toasted slivered
    almonds
1 4- to 5-pound whole lake trout *or*
    walleyed pike, dressed
Cooking oil

About 1 hour before cooking, soak the hickory chips in enough water to cover; drain. In skillet cook onion in butter till tender but not brown. Stir in apricots, orange juice, sugar, bouillon granules, and celery salt. Heat and stir to dissolve bouillon granules. Remove from heat. Add bread cubes and almonds; toss lightly. Spoon stuffing into fish cavity. Brush outside of fish with a little oil.

In covered grill arrange *slow* coals around edge of grill. Sprinkle some of the dampened hickory chips generously over coals. Center foil pan on grill, not directly over coals. Place the fish in foil pan. Close grill hood. Grill till fish flakes easily with fork, about 1¼ hours. Sprinkle hickory chips over the coals every 20 minutes. Makes 8 servings.

BARBECUED FISH

1½ pounds fresh *or* frozen fish
    fillets *or* steaks, *or* 4 pan-
    dressed fish (about 8 ounces
    each)
½ cup cooking oil
1 tablespoon Worcestershire
    sauce
½ teaspoon onion salt
⅛ teaspoon pepper
    Lemon wedges

Thaw fish, if frozen. Cut fish fillets or steaks into 4 portions. (For pan-dressed fish, wrap tails in greased foil.
Sprinkle fish cavities with salt and pepper.) Combine the
oil, Worcestershire sauce, onion salt, and pepper; mix well.
Place fish in well-greased wire grill basket. Brush fish with
oil mixture.

Grill fish over *medium-hot* coals for 5 to 8 minutes.
Brush with oil mixture; turn and brush second side. Grill
till fish flakes easily when tested with a fork, 5 to 8 minutes
more. Serve with lemon wedges. Serves 4.

CRISPY-GRILLED FISH FILLETS

¾ cup finely crushed cornflakes
⅓ cup sesame seed, toasted (1⅛-ounce container)
1 16-ounce package frozen fish
    fillets, thawed
2 tablespoons soy sauce
    Salt
    Pepper
½ cup dairy sour cream

Combine cornflake crumbs and sesame seed. Brush fish
with soy sauce. Season with salt and pepper. Spread one
side of each fillet with sour cream; press coated side in

crumb mixture. Repeat spreading with sour cream and coating other side of fillets. Place the coated fish fillets in well-greased wire grill basket. Grill fish over *medium-hot* coals about 8 minutes. Turn fish and grill till fish flakes easily with a fork, about 8 minutes more. Makes 4 servings.

SOY-MARINATED PERCH FILLETS

2   pounds fresh *or* frozen perch
       fillets
⅓ cup cooking oil
3   tablespoons soy sauce
2   tablespoons wine vinegar
2   tablespoons finely chopped onion

Thaw fish, if frozen. Place fish fillets in plastic bag set in deep bowl. Combine the cooking oil, soy sauce, wine vinegar, and finely chopped onion; mix well. Pour mixture over fish fillets in bag; close bag. Marinate fish for 30 to 60 minutes at room temperature; turn bag occasionally. Drain fish, reserving marinade.

Place fish in well-greased wire grill basket. Grill over *hot* coals for 8 to 9 minutes. Turn fish and brush with marinade. Grill till fish flakes easily when tested with a fork, 6 to 8 minutes more. Makes 6 servings.

FISH IN A BASKET

½ cup all-purpose flour
⅛ teaspoon pepper
½ teaspoon salt
4   whole pan-dressed lake *or* brook
       trout *or* perch (about 12
       ounces each)
¼ cup butter *or* margarine, melted

In a bowl combine flour, salt, and pepper. Dip fish in seasoned flour, coating thoroughly. Place the coated fish in a well-greased wire grill basket.

Grill fish over *hot* coals about 10 minutes. Turn fish and baste with melted butter. Grill till fish flakes easily when tested with a fork, about 10 minutes more; baste often with butter. Makes 4 servings.

WILD RICE-STUFFED SALMON

Hickory chips
2 cups chicken broth
¼ cup finely chopped onion
1 cup wild rice, rinsed
1 tablespoon butter *or* margarine
1 tablespoon snipped parsley
1 6-pound whole dressed salmon
Butter, melted

Soak the hickory chips in enough water to cover about 1 hour before grilling. Drain chips. In saucepan combine chicken broth and onion; bring to boiling. Add wild rice to saucepan and reduce heat. Cover; simmer till the liquid is absorbed, about 40 minutes. Stir in the 1 tablespoon butter and snipped parsley. Spoon stuffing into cavity of salmon; skewer or tie.

In covered grill arrange *slow* coals around edge of the grill. Sprinkle some of the dampened chips generously over coals. Center foil pan on grill, not directly over coals. Place fish in foil pan.

Close the grill hood. Grill till fish flakes easily when tested with a fork, 1¼ to 1½ hours. Brush fish occasionally with melted butter. Sprinkle the hickory chips over coals every 20 minutes. Makes 10 servings.

STUFFED SMOKED SALMON

Hickory chips
½ cup finely chopped celery
¼ cup chopped onion
3 tablespoons butter *or* margarine
4 cups herb-seasoned stuffing
    croutons
2 tablespoons snipped parsley
½ teaspoon grated lemon peel
1 tablespoon lemon juice
½ teaspoon salt
    Dash pepper
1 8-pound whole dressed salmon
½ cup butter *or* margarine, melted

Soak hickory chips in enough water to cover about 1 hour before grilling. Drain chips. In saucepan cook celery and onion in the 3 tablespoons butter till tender. Pour over stuffing croutons. Add parsley, lemon peel and juice, salt, and pepper. Toss together till well combined. Spoon into cavity of salmon; skewer or tie closed.

In covered grill arrange *slow* coals around edge of grill. Sprinkle some of the dampened chips over coals. Center foil pan on grill, not directly over coals. Place fish in foil pan. Close grill hood. Grill till fish flakes easily when tested with fork, 1¼ to 1½ hours. Brush fish occasionally with melted butter. Sprinkle hickory chips over coals every 20 minutes. Serves 10 to 12.

HALIBUT KABOBS

    1 12-ounce package frozen halibut
       steaks, thawed
    ¼ cup cooking oil
    ¼ cup dry vermouth
    ¼ cup lemon juice
    1 teaspoon salt
    1 teaspoon dried oregano,
       crushed
    1 small clove garlic, minced
    6 mushroom caps
    1 large green pepper
   12 cherry tomatoes

Cut fish into 1-inch pieces. In bowl combine oil, vermouth,
lemon juice, salt, oregano, and garlic. Place fish pieces in
marinade. Cover; marinate at room temperature for 1
hour. Drain fish, reserving marinade. Pour some boiling
water over mushrooms in bowl. Let stand 1 minute; drain.
Cut green pepper into 1-inch squares. On six skewers alternate fish, green pepper, and cherry tomatoes; end with
mushroom caps. Grill the kabobs over *medium* coals for 8
to 10 minutes, turning and basting frequently with marinade. Makes 6 servings.

CHARCOALED HALIBUT STEAKS

½ cup shredded unpeeled
   cucumber
½ cup dairy sour cream
¼ cup mayonnaise *or* salad dressing
1 tablespoon snipped chives
2 teaspoons lemon juice
¼ teaspoon salt
   Dash pepper
2 pounds fresh *or* frozen halibut
   steaks *or* other fish
¼ cup butter *or* margarine
1 teaspoon salt
⅛ teaspoon pepper
   Paprika

Blend shredded cucumber with sour cream, mayonnaise
or salad dressing, chives, lemon juice, the ¼ teaspoon salt,
and the dash pepper. Mix well and chill sauce.

Thaw fish, if frozen. Cut into 6 portions. Place in well-
greased wire grill basket. In saucepan melt butter; stir in
the 1 teaspoon salt and ⅛ teaspoon pepper.

Grill fish over *medium-hot* coals for 5 to 8 minutes,
brushing with butter mixture occasionally. Turn and baste
with remaining butter mixture. Grill till fish flakes easily
when tested with a fork, 5 to 8 minutes more. Sprinkle fish
with paprika and serve with chilled cucumber sauce.
Makes 6 servings.

CHARCOAL-GRILLED SHRIMP

2 pounds fresh *or* frozen large
    shrimp, shelled and deveined
½ cup olive *or* cooking oil
½ cup finely chopped onion
½ cup dry white wine
¼ cup lemon juice
¼ cup finely snipped parsley
1 tablespoon Worcestershire sauce
1 teaspoon dillweed
½ teaspoon salt

Thaw shrimp, if frozen. Combine oil, onion, wine, lemon juice, parsley, Worcestershire, dillweed, and salt. Place shrimp in plastic bag set in deep bowl. Pour marinade mixture over shrimp. Close bag. Marinate 3 to 4 hours in the refrigerator. Drain shrimp, reserving marinade.

Place shrimp in well-greased wire grill basket *or* on 24 x 18-inch piece of heavy-duty foil. Grill over *hot* coals for 15 to 20 minutes, turning basket or individual shrimp often and basting with marinade. Makes 6 servings.

BARBECUED SHRIMP KABOBS

1 8-ounce can tomato sauce
1 cup chopped onion
½ cup water
¼ cup packed brown sugar
¼ cup cooking oil
¼ cup lemon juice
3 tablespoons Worcestershire sauce
2 tablespoons prepared mustard
2 teaspoons salt
¼ teaspoon pepper
1 pound fresh *or* frozen large
   shrimp, shelled and deveined
1 15¼-ounce can pineapple chunks
1 green pepper, cut in 1-inch
   squares
2 cups cold water
1 cup regular rice
½ teaspoon salt
2 tablespoons snipped parsley

In saucepan combine tomato sauce, onion, the ½ cup water, brown sugar, cooking oil, lemon juice, Worcestershire, mustard, the 2 teaspoons salt, and pepper. Simmer, uncovered, 15 minutes, stirring once or twice; set aside. Thaw shrimp, if frozen. Drain pineapple, reserving 2 tablespoons syrup. Combine syrup with sauce mixture.

Place shrimp in plastic bag set in a deep bowl. Pour sauce mixture over shrimp; close bag. Marinate at room temperature for 2 to 3 hours. Drain, reserving sauce.

On four skewers alternately thread the shrimp, 2 pineapple chunks, and green pepper squares. Grill over *hot* coals for 5 to 8 minutes. Turn kabobs and brush with marinade. Grill till shrimp are done, 5 to 8 minutes more, basting occasionally with sauce.

Meanwhile, prepare the rice. In a saucepan combine the 2 cups cold water, rice, and ½ teaspoon salt; cover with tight-fitting lid. Bring to a rolling boil; reduce heat.

Continue cooking 14 minutes (do not lift cover). Remove from heat; let stand, covered, 10 minutes. Stir in the parsley. Serve hot shrimp kabobs over rice. Pass remaining sauce, if desired. Makes 4 servings.

FOIL-BARBECUED SHRIMP

2 pounds fresh *or* frozen large
    shrimp, shelled and deveined
6 tablespoons butter *or* margarine
½ cup snipped parsley
¾ teaspoon curry powder
1 clove garlic, minced
½ teaspoon salt
    Dash pepper

Thaw shrimp, if frozen. In saucepan melt butter; stir in parsley, curry powder, garlic, salt, and pepper. Add shrimp; stir to coat. Divide shrimp mixture equally among six 12 x 18-inch pieces of heavy-duty foil. Fold foil around shrimp, sealing the edges well.

Grill shrimp over *hot* coals about 8 minutes. Turn and grill till done, 7 to 8 minutes more. Serve in foil packages, if desired. Makes 6 servings.

SKEWERED SCALLOPS AND BACON

  8 ounces fresh *or* frozen
        unbreaded scallops (about 24)
  3 tablespoons butter *or*
        margarine, melted
  2 tablespoons lemon juice
        Dash pepper
12 bacon slices, halved crosswise
        (12 ounces)
        Paprika

Thaw scallops, if frozen. Remove any shell particles and wash thoroughly. Combine butter, lemon juice, and pepper. Pour marinade over scallops. Cover; let stand at room temperature for 30 minutes. Drain scallops; reserve marinade. In skillet partially cook bacon. Drain on paper towels and cool. Wrap each scallop with a half slice of partially cooked bacon. On six skewers thread bacon-wrapped scallops, securing bacon with skewer and allowing some space between each scallop. Sprinkle with paprika. Grill over *hot* coals, bacon side down, about 5 minutes. Turn, using spatula; baste with marinade. Grill till bacon is crisp and brown, about 5 minutes more. Serves 6.

FOIL-WRAPPED CLAMBAKE

48 soft-shelled clams in shells
 4 quarts cold water
½ cup salt
 2 2- to 2½-pound ready-to-cook
    broiler-fryer chickens,
    quartered
   Salt
   Pepper
 8 whole ears of corn
   Rockweed *or* large bunch
    parsley
 8 frozen lobster tails, thawed
    (about 2 pounds)
 1 16-ounce package frozen fish
    fillets, thawed and cut in 8
    pieces
 1 pound butter, melted

Thoroughly wash clams in shells. In a large kettle combine cold water and ⅓ cup salt. Place clams in salt-water mixture; let stand 15 minutes. Rinse well. Repeat salt-water soaking and rinsing twice more.

Break drumstick, hip, and wing joints of chickens so pieces will remain flat on grill. In covered grill place chicken pieces, skin side down, over *hot* coals. Grill about 10 minutes. Season with salt and pepper. Turn back husks of corn. Use a stiff brush to remove silk. Lay husks back in place.

Tear off sixteen 36 x 18-inch pieces of heavy-duty foil. Place 1 sheet crosswise over a second sheet. Repeat, making a total of 8 sets. Lay a handful of rockweed or parsley in center of each foil set. Cut eight 18-inch squares of cheesecloth; place 1 square atop rockweed.

For each package arrange the following on cheesecloth: 6 clams in shells, 1 precooked chicken quarter, 1 ear of corn, 1 lobster tail, and 1 piece of fish. Securely tie opposite ends of cheesecloth together. Seal opposite ends of foil together, sealing edges well.

Place foil packages, seam side up, on grill. Lower the grill hood. Grill over *hot* coals about 45 minutes.

To test for doneness: the chicken drumstick should move up and down easily in socket. Serve with individual cups of hot, melted butter. Makes 8 servings.

GRILLED ROCK LOBSTER TAILS

4   medium frozen rock lobster tails
¼   cup butter *or* margarine, melted
2   teaspoons lemon juice
1   teaspoon grated orange peel
     Generous dash *each* ground
        ginger, aromatic bitters, and
        chili powder

Thaw rock lobster tails. Cut off thin undershell membrane with kitchen scissors. Bend tail back to crack shell or insert long skewers lengthwise between shell and meat to prevent curling. (To butterfly rock lobster tails, partially thaw tails; snip through center of hard top shell with kitchen scissors. With sharp knife cut through the meat, but *not through undershell.* Spread open.)

Combine melted butter or margarine, lemon juice, orange peel, ginger, aromatic bitters, and chili powder; brush over lobster meat. With meat side up, grill lobster tails over *hot* coals for about 5 minutes. Turn, shell side up, and brush with sauce, grill till meat has lost its transparency and is opaque, 5 to 10 minutes more. Makes 4 servings.

BARBECUED KING CRAB LEGS

¼   cup butter *or* margarine, melted
¼   cup snipped parsley
¼   cup lemon juice
1   tablespoon prepared mustard
2   pounds frozen cooked king crab
     legs, thawed and shelled

Combine butter, parsley, lemon juice, mustard, and ¼ teaspoon salt. Brush the mixture on crab meat. Place crab on grill about 4 inches from *medium* coals. Brush the crab with butter mixture and turn occasionally till heated through, 5 to 8 minutes. Makes 6 servings.

GRILLED SALMON STEAKS

6 fresh *or* frozen salmon steaks *or*
    other fish steaks
½ cup salad oil
¼ cup snipped parsley
¼ cup lemon juice
2 tablespoons grated onion
½ teaspoon dry mustard
¼ teaspoon salt
    Dash pepper

Thaw fish, if frozen. Place fish in shallow dish. Combine oil, parsley, lemon juice, onion, mustard, salt, and pepper. Pour over fish. Let stand at room temperature 2 hours, turning occasionally. (*Or*, marinate, covered, in refrigerator 4 to 6 hours.) Drain, reserving marinade. Place fish in well-greased wire grill basket. Grill over *medium-hot* coals till fish is lightly browned, 5 to 8 minutes. Baste with marinade and turn. Brush again with marinade; grill till fish flakes easily when tested with a fork, 5 to 8 minutes more. Serves 6.

Basic Cuts of Fish

(A) *Dressed or pan-dressed* fish have been gutted and scaled. Usually, the head, tail, and fins have been removed. (B) *Fillets* are pieces of fish cut lengthwise from the sides of the fish. When filleting a fish, the backbone is discarded intact, so the fillets are virtually boneless. (C) *Steaks* are ⅝- to 1-inch-thick cross-section slices cut from a large dressed fish.

Sausages and Frankfurters

MUSTARD-BRUSHED BOLOGNA KABOBS

1 pound chunk bologna, cut into 1-
     inch cubes
1 15¼-ounce can pineapple chunks,
     drained
¼ cup butter *or* margarine, melted
2 tablespoons Dijon-style mustard
1 tablespoon snipped parsley
2 teaspoons lemon juice
   Dash pepper

On four skewers alternately thread bologna cubes with
pineapple chunks. Combine melted butter, mustard, parsley, lemon juice, and pepper. Brush over skewered bologna
and pineapple. Grill kabobs over *medium* coals, turning
frequently till heated through, 8 to 10 minutes. Brush the
kabobs frequently with the butter mixture. Serves 4.

QUICK FRANK KABOBS

8 frankfurters, cut into thirds
1 16-ounce can whole new
     potatoes, drained
2 medium green peppers, cut in
     pieces
¼ cup horseradish mustard
¼ cup catsup
½ envelope taco seasoning mix (about 2 tablespoons)
2 tablespoons water
2 tablespoons cooking oil
   Several drops bottled hot pepper
     sauce.

Thread frank pieces on skewers alternately with potatoes and pepper pieces. In small bowl stir together horseradish mustard, catsup, taco seasoning mix, water, oil, and hot pepper sauce. Grill kabobs over *medium* coals for 10 minutes, turning often and brushing frequently with mustard mixture. Makes 4 to 6 servings.

TANGY BARBECUED FRANKS

1 medium onion, thinly sliced
¼ cup chopped celery
¼ cup chopped green pepper
1 clove garlic, minced
¼ cup butter *or* margarine
1 10¾-ounce can condensed tomato
   soup
⅓ cup water
¼ cup packed brown sugar
2 tablespoons vinegar
2 tablespoons prepared mustard
1 tablespoon Worcestershire sauce
¼ teaspoon bottled hot pepper sauce
1 pound frankfurters (8 to 10)

In heavy 10-inch skillet over *hot* coals cook sliced onion, celery, green pepper, and garlic in butter or margarine till tender but not brown, about 10 minutes. Stir in tomato soup, water, brown sugar, vinegar, mustard, Worcestershire, and hot pepper sauce. Cover; bring to boil, allowing 15 to 20 minutes. Score franks on bias; add to hot mixture. Cook till heated through, about 10 minutes more, stirring occasionally. Makes 4 or 5 servings.

JIFFY FRANK AND CABBAGE SKILLET

2 tablespoons butter *or* margarine
2 16-ounce jars sweet-sour red
      cabbage, drained
1 12-ounce package frankfurters,
      cut in 1-inch pieces
2 medium apples, cored and
      chopped
1 small onion, chopped

In heavy skillet over *medium* coals melt butter or margarine; stir in drained cabbage, frankfurters, chopped apple, and onion. Cover; simmer mixture till onion is tender and cabbage and meat are heated through, about 20 minutes. Makes 4 servings.

SKEWERED BRATWURST

1 pound bratwurst (6 brats)
¼ cup light cream
2 tablespoons prepared mustard
½ teaspoon instant minced onion
¼ teaspoon coarsely cracked pepper
    Dash paprika
1 16-ounce can sauerkraut, drained

Cut each brat into thirds. Thread the bratwurst pieces on four skewers. For sauce, combine light cream, mustard, instant minced onion, pepper, and paprika

Grill brat pieces over *medium-hot* coals till heated through, 7 to 8 minutes; turning and brushing often with sauce. In saucepan heat sauerkraut. Serve grilled meat and sauce over hot sauerkraut. Makes 4 servings.

POLISH SAUSAGE-KRAUTERS

8 slices bacon
8 Polish sausage *or* large
   frankfurters
1 8-ounce can sauerkraut, drained
   and snipped
¼ cup chili sauce
2 tablespoons finely chopped onion
1 teaspoon sugar
1 teaspoon caraway seed

Partially cook bacon. Drain; set aside. Slit sausages *or* frankfurters, lengthwise, cutting almost to ends and only ¾ of the way through.

   Combine sauerkraut, chili sauce, onion, sugar, and caraway seed. Stuff about 2 tablespoons of the mixture into slit of each sausage or frankfurter. Wrap each with a strip of bacon; secure with wooden picks.

   Grill over *hot* coals for 10 to 12 minutes, turning frequently so bacon cooks crisp on all sides. Serves 8.

FRANK AND BEAN SKILLET

1 1¼-ounce envelope sour cream
   sauce mix
¾ cup milk
  Few drops bottled hot pepper
   sauce
1 22-ounce jar baked beans
4 or 5 frankfurters, bias-sliced
1 3-ounce can French-fried onions

In heavy skillet blend together sour cream sauce mix, milk, and hot pepper sauce. Stir in baked beans and frank pieces. Cook over *medium* coals, stirring occasionally, till mixture is heated through. Before serving, stir in about ¾ of the French-fried onions. Sprinkle remaining onions atop each serving. Makes 4 servings.

Lamb

MARINATED LEG OF LAMB

1 5- to 6-pound leg of lamb
½ cup lemon juice
½ cup cooking oil
¼ cup finely chopped onion
2 tablespoons finely snipped
   parsley
1 teaspoon salt
½ teaspoon dried thyme, crushed
½ teaspoon dried basil, crushed
¼ teaspoon dried tarragon, crushed

Have meatman bone leg of lamb and slit lengthwise so you can spread it flat on grill like a thick steak. Combine lemon juice, oil, onion, parsley, salt, thyme, basil, and tarragon. Place lamb in large plastic bag set in deep bowl. Pour lemon juice mixture over lamb; close bag. Refrigerate 4 to 6 hours, turning bag occasionally to coat lamb evenly. Drain lamb, reserving marinade.

Insert two long skewers through meat at right angles making a +, or place meat in a wire grill basket. (This makes for easy turning of meat and keeps meat from curling during cooking.) Grill over *medium* coals, turning every 15 minutes, till desired doneness, about 1½ hours for medium or 2 hours for well-done. Baste frequently with reserved marinade. Place lamb on carving board; remove from basket or remove skewers. Cut lamb across grain into thin slices. Makes 8 to 10 servings.

Note: This marinade is equally good on bone-in leg of lamb (see chart on pages 4-5 for timings).

APRICOT LAMB KABOBS

½ cup chopped onion
1 small clove garlic, minced
2 tablespoons cooking oil
1 17-ounce can apricot halves
3 tablespoons vinegar
2 tablespoons brown sugar
½ teaspoon curry powder
  Dash bottled hot pepper sauce
1 teaspoon salt
1½ pounds boneless lamb, cut in 1½-inch cubes

In saucepan cook onion and garlic in hot oil till onion is tender but not brown. Place cooked onion, garlic, oil, apricots, vinegar, brown sugar, curry powder, hot pepper sauce, and 1 teaspoon salt in blender container. Cover; blend till smooth. Return mixture to saucepan; simmer, covered, 10 minutes. Cool. Pour mixture over lamb; cover and refrigerate overnight, turning meat occasionally. Drain, reserving marinade. Thread meat on six skewers; grill over *hot* coals for 15 to 20 minutes, turning often. Heat marinade; pass with kabobs. Makes 6 servings.

Balancing Meat
on a Spit

Meat "done to a turn" on a rotisserie is easy once you learn how to balance the meat. To mount boneless roasts, insert the spit rod through the center of the roast and secure with holding forks. Test the balance by holding one end of rod in the palm of each hand and turning gently. If the meat flops or turns unevenly, readjust holding forks or rod as necessary. Bone-in meat is harder to balance. To offset the bone's weight, insert the rod diagonally. Adjust the holding forks and test the balance as above.

SAUCY LAMB RIBLETS

3 to 4 pounds lamb riblets, cut in
    serving-size pieces
½ cup chopped onion
1 tablespoon cooking oil
¾ cup catsup
¼ cup water
3 tablespoons Worcestershire sauce
2 tablespoons brown sugar
2 tablespoons vinegar
¾ teaspoon salt
    Dash bottled hot pepper sauce

Trim excess fat from riblets. Cook riblets, covered, in boiling salted water till tender, 1 to 1¼ hours. Drain. Meanwhile, cook onion in oil till tender. Add catsup, water, Worcestershire, brown sugar, vinegar, salt, and hot pepper sauce; heat through.

Grill riblets over *medium-hot* coals for 10 to 15 minutes; turn. Grill 10 to 15 minutes. Brush riblets with catsup mixture; continue grilling till riblets are hot and glazed, 10 to 15 minutes more. Reheat catsup mixture. Brush on riblets before serving; pass with meat. Makes 4 servings.

HERBED LAMB-VEGETABLE KABOBS

½ cup cooking oil
½ cup chopped onion
¼ cup snipped parsley
¼ cup lemon juice
1 teaspoon salt
1 teaspoon dried marjoram,
    crushed
1 teaspoon dried thyme, crushed
1 clove garlic, minced
½ teaspoon pepper
2 pounds boneless lamb, cut in 1-
    inch cubes
  Onion wedges
  Green pepper squares
  Sweet red pepper squares

Combine cooking oil, onion, parsley, lemon juice, salt,
marjoram, thyme, garlic, and pepper; stir in lamb. Cover;
refrigerate 6 to 8 hours, stirring occasionally. Drain lamb,
reserving marinade. Cook wedges of onion in water till
tender; drain.

    Thread six skewers with lamb cubes, onion wedges,
green pepper squares, and sweet red pepper squares. Grill
over *hot* coals for 10 to 12 minutes; turn and brush often
with reserved marinade. Serves 6.

ARMENIAN-ITALIAN LAMB CHOPS

1 cup tomato juice
½ cup finely chopped onion
½ cup lemon juice
¼ cup finely chopped dill pickle
¼ cup finely chopped green pepper
2 tablespoons sugar
1 teaspoon salt
1 teaspoon ground cumin
1 teaspoon dried marjoram,
    crushed
¼ teaspoon pepper
4 teaspoons cornstarch
2 tablespoons cold water
6 lamb shoulder chops, cut 1 inch
    thick

In saucepan combine tomato juice, onion, lemon juice, pickle, green pepper, sugar, salt, cumin, marjoram, and ¼ teaspoon pepper. Simmer, covered, till onion and green pepper are tender, about 10 minutes. Blend cornstarch and cold water; stir into sauce. Cook and stir till thickened.

Grill lamb chops over *medium* coals for 10 to 12 minutes. Turn chops and grill till done, 10 to 12 minutes more, brushing frequently with sauce. (Keep sauce warm by placing it in small saucepan on grill.) Pass the remaining sauce with the lamb chops. Makes 6 servings.

BARBECUE SAUCES AND MARINADES

Want to perk up and improve the smoky flavor of meat cooking on the grill? All you need is a tangy basting sauce or a savory marinade to bring out the flavors of barbecued food. And this chapter features some of the best. Once you have basted a just-right sauce on beef, then next time try it on grilled pork, lamb, poultry, or seafood. Be sure to try the special relishes with different barbecued meats, and savor the flavor combinations.

Sauces and Relishes

SNAPPY BARBECUE SAUCE

1 cup catsup
1 cup water
¼ cup vinegar
1 tablespoon sugar
1 tablespoon Worcestershire sauce
1 teaspoon salt
1 teaspoon celery seed
2 or 3 dashes bottled hot pepper
   sauce

In saucepan combine catsup, water, vinegar, sugar, Worcestershire, salt, celery seed, and bottled hot pepper sauce. Bring the mixture to boiling; reduce heat and simmer, uncovered, for 30 minutes. Use to baste pork or beef ribs during last 15 to 20 minutes of barbecuing. Pass remaining sauce. Makes about 2 cups.

EASY BARBECUE SAUCE

1 14-ounce bottle hot-style catsup
3 tablespoons vinegar
2 teaspoons celery seed
1 clove garlic, halved

Combine catsup, vinegar, celery seed, and garlic.
Refrigerate, covered, for several hours. Remove garlic.
Use to baste hamburgers or beef during last 10 minutes of
barbecuing. Makes about 1½ cups sauce.

WESTERN HOT SAUCE

½ cup catsup
¼ cup water
¼ cup finely chopped onion
3 tablespoons red wine vinegar
2 tablespoons cooking oil
2 teaspoons brown sugar
2 teaspoons Worcestershire sauce
2 teaspoons whole mustard seed
1 teaspoon paprika
½ teaspoon dried oregano, crushed
½ teaspoon chili powder
¼ teaspoon salt
⅛ teaspoon ground cloves
1 bay leaf
1 clove garlic, minced

In saucepan combine catsup, water, onion, vinegar, oil,
brown sugar, Worcestershire, mustard seed, paprika,
oregano, chili powder, salt, cloves, bay leaf, and garlic.
Bring mixture to boiling; reduce heat and simmer, uncovered, for 10 minutes, stirring once or twice. Discard bay
leaf. Use to baste hamburgers or ribs during last 10 to 15
minutes of barbecuing. Makes about 1½ cups.

DURANGO SAUCE

1 16-ounce can pork and beans in
    tomato sauce
1 8-ounce can tomato sauce
½ cup water
1 1¼-ounce envelope chili
    seasoning mix
1 teaspoon Worcestershire sauce

In blender container combine pork and beans in tomato sauce, tomato sauce, water, chili seasoning mix, and Worcestershire sauce. Cover and blend the mixture till smooth. Use sauce to baste pork chops, steaks, or hamburgers during last 5 minutes of barbecuing. Heat remaining sauce to pass. Makes 2½ cups.

MOLASSES-ORANGE BARBECUE SAUCE

1 10¾-ounce can condensed
    tomato soup
1 8-ounce can tomato sauce
½ cup light molasses
½ cup vinegar
½ cup packed brown sugar
¼ cup cooking oil
1 tablespoon instant minced
    onion.
1 tablespoon seasoned salt
1 tablespoon dry mustard
1 tablespoon Worcestershire
    sauce
1 tablespoon finely shredded
    orange peel
1½ teaspoons paprika
½ teaspoon pepper
¼ teaspoon garlic powder

In medium saucepan combine soup, tomato sauce, molasses, vinegar, brown sugar, oil, onion, salt, mustard, Worcestershire, peel, paprika, pepper and garlic powder. Bring to boiling; reduce heat and simmer, uncovered, for 20 minutes. Use to baste poultry or beef during last 15 minutes of barbecuing. Makes about 3½ cups sauce.

CHILI BARBECUE SAUCE

½ cup chili sauce
2 tablespoons cooking oil
2 tablespoons pineapple *or* orange
    juice
1 tablespoon brown sugar
   Dash bottled hot pepper sauce

Combine chili sauce, oil, pineapple or orange juice, brown sugar, and pepper sauce; mix well. Use as a marinade or brush over seafood, chicken, or pork during last 5 to 10 minutes of barbecuing. Makes about ¾ cup.

BIG-BATCH BARBECUE SAUCE

½ cup finely chopped celery
½ cup finely chopped green pepper
1 clove garlic, minced
¼ cup butter *or* margarine
4 cups catsup
1 10½-ounce can condensed onion
    soup
1 10½-ounce can condensed
    chicken gumbo soup
2 tablespoons vinegar
½ teaspoon bottled hot pepper sauce
½ cup water
1 cup dry white wine

In large saucepan cook celery, green pepper, and garlic in butter or margarine till tender. Stir in catsup, soups, vinegar, hot pepper sauce, and ½ cup water. Simmer mixture 30 minutes, stirring occasionally. Stir in wine. Pour into 1- or 2-cup freezer containers. Seal, label, and freeze. To use, thaw the sauce. Use to baste chicken, frankfurters, ribs, or steaks the last 10 to 15 minutes of barbecuing. Heat the remaining sauce to pass, if desired. Makes 8 cups sauce.

PINEAPPLE-ORANGE GLAZE

½ of a 6-ounce can frozen
    pineapple juice concentrate
¼ cup orange marmalade
2 tablespoons bottled steak sauce

In saucepan combine pineapple concentrate, marmalade, and steak sauce. Cook and stir the mixture till heated through. Use to baste poultry or pork during the last 10 to 15 minutes of barbecuing. Makes about ¾ cup.

TARRAGON-CIDER BASTING SAUCE

½ cup apple cider *or* juice
½ cup vinegar
¼ cup sliced green onion with tops
2 tablespoons butter *or* margarine
2 tablespoons bottled steak sauce
2 tablespoons honey
1 teaspoon salt
1 teaspoon dried tarragon, crushed
¼ teaspoon pepper

In a 1½-quart saucepan combine cider, vinegar, onion, butter, steak sauce, honey, salt, tarragon, and pepper. Bring to boiling; simmer, uncovered, for 20 minutes, stirring mixture occasionally. Use as a meat marinade or use to baste chicken, beef, pork, or fish during last 15 to 20 minutes of barbecuing. Heat and pass the remaining sauce. Makes about ¾ cups sauce.

COFFEE-SOY GLAZE

½ cup packed brown sugar
1 tablespoon cornstarch
⅔ cup cold strong coffee
¼ cup soy sauce
3 tablespoons wine vinegar

In a small saucepan blend together the brown sugar and cornstarch. Add coffee, soy sauce, and vinegar; mix well. Cook and stir mixture till thickened and bubbly. Use to baste spareribs or pork chops during the last 15 minutes of barbecuing. Makes about 1 cup sauce.

SOY-LEMON BASTING SAUCE

1 tablespoon brown sugar
1 teaspoon cornstarch
2 tablespoons lemon juice
2 tablespoons soy sauce
2 tablespoons water
2 tablespoons sliced green onion
     with tops
1 tablespoon butter *or* margarine
1 clove garlic, minced

In saucepan blend brown sugar and cornstarch. Stir in lemon juice, soy sauce, and water. Add onion, butter, and garlic. Cook and stir till thickened and bubbly. Use to baste poultry or fish during last 15 minutes of barbecuing. Makes about ½ cup.

SEASONED BUTTER LOG

¼ cup butter, softened
2 tablespoons braunschweiger
2 teaspoons lemon juice
¼ teaspoon dried basil, crushed
  Paprika

Blend together softened butter, braunschweiger, lemon juice, and basil. Shape into a 4-inch log on waxed paper. Roll log in paprika to coat. Chill till firm. Slice butter log and serve with grilled steaks.

CARAWAY-CHEESE SPREAD

1 3-ounce package cream cheese,
  softened
1 tablespoon butter, softened
1 teaspoon caraway seed
1 teaspoon prepared mustard

In a small bowl blend together cream cheese and softened butter. Stir in caraway seed and mustard. Spread atop grilled hamburgers. Makes about ½ cup.

ZESTY SAUERKRAUT RELISH

½ cup sugar
½ cup vinegar
1 teaspoon prepared mustard
¼ teaspoon garlic powder
¼ teaspoon pepper
1 16-ounce can sauerkraut, drained
⅓ cup chopped sweet red *or* green pepper
⅓ cup chopped onion
⅓ cup chopped cucumber

In saucepan heat sugar and vinegar till sugar is dissolved; stir occasionally. Stir in mustard, garlic powder, and pepper. Cool. Combine drained sauerkraut, red or green pepper, onion, and cucumber; stir together with the vinegar mixture. Cover and chill the relish till needed. Makes about 3 cups relish.

CUCUMBER RELISH

3 large tomatoes, chopped
1 medium cucumber, peeled,
    seeded, and chopped (1 cup)
¼ cup chopped fresh coriander leaves
3 tablespoons finely chopped onion
¼ teaspoon finely chopped canned green chili peppers
1 tablespoon lemon juice
½ teaspoon salt

Combine tomatoes, cucumber, coriander leaves, onion, and chili peppers. Stir together lemon juice and salt. Add to the vegetable mixture and mix well. Cover and chill till needed. Makes about 2⅓ cups relish.

SANDWICH COLESLAW

2 cups finely shredded cabbage
⅓ cup thinly sliced green onion with tops
¼ cup snipped parsley
2 tablespoons sugar
3 tablespoons vinegar
1 teaspoon salt
½ teaspoon celery seed
   Dash bottled hot pepper sauce

Combine the shredded cabbage, green onion, and parsley. Stir together sugar, vinegar, salt, celery seed, and hot pepper sauce. Pour over cabbage mixture and toss. Cover and chill till needed. Makes about 2 cups relish.

RATATOUILLE RELISH

2 medium green peppers, stems
      and seeds removed
2 tomatoes, cored
1 medium onion
1 medium zucchini
½ of a small eggplant, peeled
2 tablespoons salt
1 cup sugar
1 cup vinegar
1 cup water
1 teaspoon whole mustard seed
¾ teaspoon celery seed
¼ teaspoon fines herbs

Using coarse blade of food chopper, grind peppers, tomatoes, onion, zucchini, and eggplant. Stir salt into vegetables. Cover; refrigerate and let stand overnight. Rinse and drain vegetables. In saucepan combine sugar, vinegar, water, mustard seed, celery seed, and fines herbs. Stir in vegetables. Bring mixture to boiling; reduce heat and simmer 5 minutes, stirring frequently. Cool. Cover and chill till needed. Makes about 4 cups relish.

RED PEPPER RELISH

6 sweet red peppers (about 1½ pounds)
2 medium onions, quartered
¾ cup sugar
¾ cup vinegar
1½ teaspoons salt

Remove stems and seeds from red peppers. Using coarse blade of food chopper, grind peppers and onions, reserving juices. In Dutch oven or large saucepan combine peppers and onions and reserved juices. Stir in sugar, vinegar, and salt. Bring to boiling; boil gently, uncovered, for 20 to 25 minutes. Cool; cover and chill till needed. Makes about 2 cups relish.

Marinades

ARMENIAN HERB MARINADE

½ cup olive *or* cooking oil
½ cup chopped onion
½ cup tomato juice
¼ cup lemon juice
¼ cup snipped parsley
1 teaspoon salt
1 teaspoon dried marjoram, crushed
1 teaspoon dried thyme, crushed
½ teaspoon pepper
1 clove garlic, minced

Combine oil, chopped onion, tomato juice, lemon juice, parsley, salt, marjoram, thyme, pepper, and garlic. Place lamb, pork, or chicken in a plastic bag set in a deep bowl or a shallow baking dish. Pour marinade mixture over meat. Close bag or cover dish; refrigerate 4 to 6 hours or overnight. Turn the bag or spoon marinade over the meat occasionally to coat evenly. Makes 1¾ cups (enough for 3 to 4 pounds meat.)

SAVORY WINE MARINADE

1 small onion
½ cup cooking oil
½ cup white wine
¼ cup lime juice *or* lemon juice
2 tablespoons snipped parsley
½ teaspoon salt
¼ teaspoon bottled hot pepper sauce

Thinly slice the onion; separate into rings. Combine oil, wine, lime juice, parsley, salt, and pepper sauce; add onion. Place fish or chicken in a plastic bag set in a deep bowl or a shallow baking dish. Pour marinade mixture over meat. Close bag or cover dish; refrigerate for 4 to 6 hours or overnight. Turn the bag or spoon marinade over the meat occasionally to coat evenly. Makes about 1½ cups (enough for 3 pounds meat).

TERIYAKI MARINADE

¼ cup cooking oil
¼ cup soy sauce
¼ cup dry sherry
1 tablespoon grated fresh
    gingerroot *or* 1 teaspoon
    ground ginger
1 clove garlic, minced
2 tablespoons molasses

Combine oil, soy sauce, dry sherry, ginger, and garlic. Place chicken, beef, or pork in plastic bag set in deep bowl or a shallow baking dish. Pour marinade mixture over meat. Close bag or cover dish; refrigerate 4 to 6 hours or overnight. Turn bag or spoon marinade over meat occasionally to coat evenly. Drain, reserving marinade. Stir in molasses. Use to baste meat during last 10 minutes of barbecuing. Makes about 1 cup (enough for 2 pounds meat).

HERB-SEASONED MARINADE

¼ cup cooking oil
¼ cup wine vinegar
¼ cup finely chopped onion
1 tablespoon Worcestershire sauce
½ teaspoon dried basil, crushed
½ teaspoon dried rosemary, crushed
¼ teaspoon pepper
⅛ teaspoon bottled hot pepper
    sauce
½ teaspoon salt

Combine oil, vinegar, onion, Worcestershire, basil, rosemary, pepper, hot pepper sauce, and ½ teaspoon salt. Place beef, pork, or chicken in a plastic bag set in a deep bowl or a shallow baking dish. Pour marinade mixture over meat. Close bag or cover dish; refrigerate 4 to 6 hours or overnight. Turn bag or spoon marinade over meat occasionally to coat evenly. Makes about ¾ cup (enough for 2 pounds meat).

GRILL-SIDE RECIPES

Meat grilled to flavor perfection is only the beginning of an outstanding backyard menu. It's the tantalizing accompaniments that really make a good meal great. Each of the recipes in this chapter, whether it's an appetizer hot off the grill or one of the many vegetables, breads, or desserts, will keep your family and friends coming back for more. All of these recipes cook right on the grill along with the meat while it barbecues.

Vegetables

SWEET HERBED TOMATOES

6 medium tomatoes, peeled
2 medium cucumbers, scored and
      thinly sliced (3½ cups)
½ cup salad oil
¼ cup dry white wine
¼ cup white wine vinegar
2 tablespoons snipped chives
1 tablespoon snipped parsley
1 tablespoon sugar
1 tablespoon dried salad herbs,
      crushed
⅛ teaspoon freshly ground pepper
1 teaspoon salt

Lightly sprinkle tomatoes with salt. In large deep bowl place whole tomatoes and sliced cucumbers. In screw-top jar combine salad oil, dry white wine, white wine vinegar, chives, parsley, sugar, salad herbs, pepper, and 1 teaspoon salt; cover and shake vigorously. Pour over vegetables.

Cover and chill several hours or overnight to thoroughly blend flavors. Turn tomatoes once or twice.

Remove tomatoes, reserving cucumbers in marinade. Wrap *each* tomato in a 6-inch square of heavy-duty foil. Grill over *medium* coals till heated through, about 20 minutes, turning once. Drain cucumbers; reserve marinade to store leftovers. Serve cucumbers atop tomatoes. Serves 6.

GRILLED ACORN SQUASH

3 medium acorn squash
2 tablespoons butter *or* margarine
2 tablespoons brown sugar
2 tablespoons water
   Brown sugar
1 apple, cut into wedges

Rinse squash. Cut in half lengthwise; remove seeds. Prick inside with tines of fork; season cavities with salt and pepper. Add *1 teaspoon* each of butter, brown sugar, and water to each squash. Wrap each half, cut side up, in 12 x 18-inch piece of heavy-duty foil; seal securely. Place cut side up on grill. Grill over *medium* coals till tender, 50 to 60 minutes. Open; stir to fluff squash; sprinkle with additional brown sugar. Top with wedges. Serves 6.

CHEESY POTATO-CARROT FOIL BAKE

4 slices bacon
3 large potatoes
3 medium carrots, shredded
¼ cup sliced green onion with tops
   Salt
   Pepper
¼ cup butter *or* margarine
½ teaspoon caraway seed
1 cup shredded Monterey Jack
      cheese (4 ounces)

Cook bacon till crisp; drain and crumble. Set aside. Tear off a 36 x 18-inch piece of heavy-duty foil. Fold in half to make an 18-inch square. Fold up sides, using fist to form a pouch. Thinly slice potatoes into pouch; add carrots and green onion. Sprinkle with salt and pepper; dot with butter and sprinkle with caraway. Fold edges of foil to seal pouch securely, leaving space for expansion of steam. Grill over *slow* coals till done, 55 to 60 minutes; turn several times. Open package; stir in crumbled bacon and cheese. Close pouch; return to grill till cheese melts, about 1 minute. Serves 6.

VEGETABLES ON A STICK

6 small onions
5 small pattypan squash
2 sweet red peppers
¼ cup butter *or* margarine
¼ teaspoon salt
   Dash pepper

Cook onions in small amount of boiling salted water till nearly tender, about 25 minutes; drain. Quarter squash; cut red peppers into large squares. In small saucepan heat butter with salt and pepper till butter melts.

On four skewers alternately thread vegetables. Grill over *medium* coals till done, 20 to 25 minutes; turning and brushing often with butter sauce. Serves 4.

HERBED ONION SLICES

3 tablespoons butter
1 tablespoon brown sugar
½ teaspoon salt
2 large onions, cut into ½-inch
     slices
¼ cup finely chopped celery
2 tablespoons finely snipped
     parsley
2 tablespoons grated Parmesan
     cheese
¼ teaspoon dried oregano, crushed

In large heavy skillet melt butter over *medium-slow* coals;
stir in brown sugar, ½ teaspoon salt, and dash pepper. Place
onion slices in a single layer in butter mixture. Sprinkle
celery over all. Cover; cook slowly for 10 minutes. Turn
onion slices; sprinkle with parsley, Parmesan, and oregano.
Cook, covered, 10 minutes more. Serves 4.

HERBED-SEASONED VEGETABLES

8 small onions
4 large carrots, cut in 1½-inch
     pieces
4 small pattypan squash
2 green peppers
¼ cup butter, melted
¼ teaspoon dried rosemary, crushed
¼ teaspoon dried marjoram, crushed
¼ teaspoon salt

In saucepan cook onions and carrots in small amount of
boiling salted water till nearly tender, about 20 minutes;
drain. Cut squash into 1-inch wedges; cut peppers into 1-
inch squares. Combine butter, rosemary, marjoram, ¼ teaspoon salt, and dash pepper.

On four skewers alternately thread vegetables. Grill over *medium* coals till done, about 20 minutes; turn and brush frequently with butter mixture. Serves 4.

CORN WITH CHIVE SAUCE

6 ears corn
½ cup chopped celery
1 2-ounce jar sliced pimiento,
   chopped
1 4-ounce container whipped
   cream cheese with chives
2 tablespoons milk
¼ teaspoon salt
  Dash pepper

Using a sharp knife, cut off tips of corn kernels; carefully scrape cobs with dull edge of knife. Combine corn, celery, pimiento, cheese, milk, salt, and pepper; mix well.

Tear off a 36 x 18-inch piece of heavy-duty foil. Fold in half to make an 18-inch square; fold up sides slightly. Spoon corn mixture onto center of foil. Fold edges of foil to seal securely, leaving space for exapnsion of steam. Grill over *medium-hot* coals till tender, about 40 minutes; turn occasionally. Serves 6.

EGGPLANT-TOMATO STACK-UPS

12 slices eggplant, cut ½-inch thick
   Seasoned salt
 3 to 4 tablespoons butter *or*
   margarine
 6 thick slices tomato
 6 slices process Swiss cheese,
   halved

Sprinkle eggplant with seasoned salt. In skillet fry eggplant on range top on both sides in butter till nearly tender, about 5 minutes. Tear off six 6-inch squares of heavy-duty foil; place *one* eggplant slice on *each* piece of foil. Top each with *one* tomato slice and a *half slice* cheese; cover with remaining eggplant slices, then remaining cheese. Seal foil packets loosely. Grill over *medium* coals till heated through, 5 to 8 minutes. Serves 6.

CHEESE-TOPPED TOMATOES

2 tomatoes
¾ cup soft bread crumbs
½ cup shredded sharp American cheese (2 ounces)
2 tablespoons butter, melted
2 tablespoons snipped parsley

Slice each tomato in half crosswise. Sprinkle cut surfaces with a little salt and pepper. Combine bread crumbs, cheese, and butter; sprinkle over tomatoes. Garnish with parsley. Wrap each tomato half loosely in a 6-inch square of heavy-duty foil. Grill over *medium-hot* coals till heated through, 15 to 20 minutes. Makes 4 servings.

CHEESE-SAUCED PEAS AND MUSHROOMS

1 10-ounce package frozen peas
    with sliced mushrooms
½ cup light cream
¼ cup shredded process Swiss cheese *or*
    American cheese
2 tablespoons snipped chives
1 clove garlic, minced

Tear off a 36 x 18-inch piece of heavy-duty foil. Fold in half to make an 18-inch square. Fold up sides, using fist to make a pouch. Place frozen peas with sliced mushrooms in pouch. Add light cream, cheese, chives, garlic, dash salt, and dash pepper. Fold edges of foil to seal pouch securely, leaving space for expansion of steam. Grill over *medium-hot* coals till heated through, about 20 minutes. Transfer to serving bowl. Makes 4 servings.

BROCCOLI IN FOIL

2 10-ounce packages frozen
    broccoli spears
  Seasoned salt
  Pepper
3 tablespoons water
2 tablespoons butter *or* margarine
  Lemon slices

Tear off a 36 x 18-inch piece of heavy-duty foil. Fold in half
to make an 18-inch square. Fold up sides, using fist to form
pouch. Place frozen broccoli in center of pouch. Sprinkle
with seasoned salt and pepper. Add water; dot with butter.
Fold edges of foil to seal securely, leaving space for expansion of steam. Grill over *medium-slow* coals till done,
about 60 minutes, turn often. Garnish with lemon slices.
Makes 6 servings.

YELLOW LEMON RICE

1⅓ cups quick-cooking rice
1⅓ cups water
  2 tablespoons lemon juice
  2 tablespoons ground turmeric
  1 teaspoon mustard seed
  ¾ teaspoon salt
  2 tablespoons butter *or* margarine

Tear off a 36 x 18-inch piece of heavy-duty foil. Fold in half
to make an 18-inch square. Fold up sides, using fist to form
a pouch. In bowl thoroughly combine rice, water, lemon
juice, ground turmeric, mustard seed, and salt. Place mixture in pouch; dot with butter. Fold edges of foil to seal
pouch securely. Grill over *medium-hot* coals till done, 15 to
20 minutes. Before serving, open pouch and fluff rice with
a fork. Makes 4 servings.

ZUCCHINI FRITTERS

⅓ cup packaged biscuit mix
¼ cup grated Parmesan cheese
⅛ teaspoon pepper
2 slightly beaten eggs
2 cups shredded unpeeled zucchini
    (2 medium)
2 tablespoons butter

In bowl stir together biscuit mix, Parmesan cheese, and pepper. Stir in beaten eggs just till mixture is moistened. Fold in zucchini. In large heavy skillet or griddle melt butter over *medium-hot* coals. Using 2 tablespoons mixture for each fritter, cook four at a time till browned, 4 to 5 minutes on each side. Keep warm while cooking remaining zucchini fritters. Makes 6 servings.

MARINATED VEGETABLE KABOBS

1 10-ounce package frozen Brussel
    sprouts
½ cup salad oil
¼ cup vinegar
1 clove garlic, minced
1 teaspoon celery seed
1 teaspoon dried parsley flakes,
    crushed
½ teaspoon salt
¼ teaspoon dried basil, crushed
¼ teaspoon pepper
4 tomatoes, cut in wedges
4 ounces fresh mushrooms
2 small cucumbers, cut in 1-inch
    slices

Cook Brussels sprouts in boiling salted water till barely tender, about 5 minutes; drain. Meanwhile, in screw-top jar combine salad oil, vinegar, garlic, celery seed, parsley flakes, salt, basil, and pepper; cover and shake well. Place Brussels sprouts, tomatoes, mushrooms, and cucumbers in plastic bag set in deep bowl. Pour marinade mixture over vegetables. Close bag; refrigerate 6 to 8 hours or overnight, stirring occasionally. Drain vegetables, reserving marinade. On six skewers thread Brussels sprouts, tomatoes, mushrooms, and cucumbers. Grill over *medium* coals till heated through, 15 to 20 minutes, turning and brushing frequently with marinade mixture. Serves 6.

ROASTED CORN ON THE COB

½ cup butter *or* margarine,
    softened
1 teaspoon salt
½ teaspoon dried rosemary, crushed
½ teaspoon dried marjoram, crushed
6 ears corn

Cream together butter and salt till fluffy. Combine herbs and blend into butter. Keep mixture at room temperature for 1 hour to blend flavors. Turn back husks of corn; remove silks with stiff brush. Place each ear on a piece of heavy-duty foil. Spread corn with about *1 tablespoon* of the butter. Lay husks back in position. Wrap corn securely. Roast ears directly on *hot* coals; turn frequently till corn is tender, 12 to 15 minutes. Or, on covered grill with an elevated rack, roast corn according to manufacturer's directions. Serves 6.

ANISE CORN

1 12-ounce can whole kernel corn,
   drained
2 tablespoons butter *or* margarine
¼ teaspoon anise seed, crushed
   Dash salt
   Dash pepper

Tear off a 36 x 18-inch piece of heavy-duty foil. Fold in half to make an 18-inch square. Fold up sides, using fist to make a pouch. Place corn in pouch; dot with butter. Sprinkle anise seed over all; add salt and pepper. Fold edges of foil to seal pouch securely, leaving space for expansion of steam. Grill over *medium-hot* coals till heated through, 15 to 20 minutes. Makes 4 servings.

Frozen Vegetables
Hot off the Grill

Utilize your grill to best advantage by cooking frozen vegetables alongside the meat. It's easy. Here's how: Tear off a 36 x 18-inch piece of heavy-duty foil. Fold in half to make an 18-inch square. Fold up sides, using fist to form pouch. Place one 10-ounce package of frozen vegetables in center of pouch. Season with salt and pepper; top with a pat of butter or margarine. Fold edges of foil to seal pouch securely, leaving space for expansion of steam. Grill over *medium-hot* coals till vegetables are cooked (allow about 20 minutes for peas and other small vegetables; allow longer for larger vegetables). Turn package frequently.

CHEESY EGGPLANT SLICES

1 medium eggplant, peeled and
   sliced ¾ inch thick (about 1
   pound)
¼ cup butter *or* margarine, melted
½ cup finely crushed round cheese
   crackers (16 crackers)
4 slices mozzarella *or* Swiss cheese,
   cut in half diagonally

Tear off four 18 x 18-inch pieces of heavy-duty foil.
Sprinkle eggplant slices with salt and pepper. Dip each
eggplant slice into melted butter, then into crushed cheese
crackers. Place *two* slices of eggplant on *each* square of
foil. Wrap foil loosely around eggplant, sealing edges securely,. Grill packets over *medium* coals about 10 minutes.
Turn and grill till eggplant is done, 6 to 7 minutes more.
Open foil and top *each* eggplant slice with *one* cheese tri-
angle. Makes 4 servings.

WHOLE GRILLED POTATOES

6 potatoes
   Cooking oil
   Shredded Swiss cheese
   Sliced green onion with tops

Tear off six 6 x 6-inch pieces of heavy-duty foil. Brush potatoes with some cooking oil. Wrap *one* potato in *each* 6-inch
square of foil. Place on covered grill; lower the hood. Grill
over *medium-slow* coals till tender, 1½ to 2 hours, turning
occasionally. Open potatoes with tines of fork and push
ends to fluff. Top with shredded cheese and sliced green
onion. Makes 6 servings.

MICROWAVE COOKERY

HOW TO COOK IN YOUR MICROWAVE OVEN

Cooking in your microwave oven is very similar to the conventional way. You can bake, roast, stew, steam, poach, boil, fry, sear, sauté and grill foods in your microwave oven. You'll find when conventional recipes call for a double-boiler, you can cook successfully, with no scorching or lumping, and without that second container of water. However, the techniques for doing these things in your microwave oven differ from the conventional methods.

A microwave oven requires no preheating. You can cook frozen convenience foods without defrosting them first. In fact, many cooks use their microwave ovens only for heating frozen convenience foods and heating leftovers. But the microwave can do so much more.

It does a superb job of cooking many foods from "scratch." Microwave-cooked fresh vegetables are beautiful and retain their garden color and flavor because they are cooked with very little water. Most casseroles can be cooked in about 20 minutes. Your microwave oven is great for defrosting meats and other foods. If friends drop in unexpectedly, you can still serve a delicious meal—even if it means defrosting the roast.

LOW—MEDIUM—HIGH

There are five buttons across the top of some control panels: OFF, LOW, MEDIUM, HIGH and BROWN.

LOW, MEDIUM, and HIGH control how fast the food is cooked. Some foods, because of their delicate make-up, need to be cooked slowly to avoid toughening. These foods use MEDIUM or LOW. Ovens with only one cooking speed are always on the HIGH setting.

Selecting the correct power level and time is very important in microwave cooking.

APPETIZER MEATBALLS

1 egg, slightly beaten
⅓ cup milk
⅓ cup fine, dry bread crumbs
1 tablespoon instant minced onion
1 teaspoon salt
1 teaspoon sugar
¼ teaspoon allspice
1 lb. lean ground meat

Combine ingredients and form into 1-inch balls. Place on wire rack in 7½" x 12" utility dish. Raise shelf. Cook on High for 4 to 6 minutes. Brown 3 to 5 minutes. Makes about 25 meatballs.

CHEESE PUFFS

3 green onions, finely chopped
1 cup grated cheddar cheese
½ cup mayonnaise
24 toast rounds

Combine green onions with cheese and mayonnaise. Spread on toast rounds. In 8¼-inch shallow baking dish heat half the rounds on Medium for 1½ to 2½ minutes or until bubbly. Turn baking dish once during cooking. Repeat with remaining puffs. Serve hot. Makes 24 appetizers.

STUFFED MUSHROOMS

4 slices bacon, diced
¼ cup minced onion
2 tablespoons minced green pepper
½ teaspoon salt
½ teaspoon Worcestershire sauce
1 (3-oz.) pkg. cream cheese
1 lb. small fresh mushrooms
½ cup soft bread crumbs
1 tablespoon butter or margarine

Combine bacon, onion, and green pepper in 4-cup measure. Cover with paper towel. Cook on High for 4 minutes, stirring once. Pour off fat. Mix in salt, Worcestershire sauce and cream cheese. Wash and dry mushrooms. Remove stems. Chop stems and add to bacon mixture. Fill mushrooms with bacon mixture. In 2-cup measure, heat bread crumbs and butter or margarine on High for 1 minute. Stir until well mixed. Press buttered crumbs on top of stuffed mushrooms. Place half the mushrooms in 6" x 10" baking dish, filling side up. Cook on High for 1 to 2 minutes. Repeat with remaining mushrooms. Makes about 50 stuffed mushrooms.

BACON-WRAPPED WATER CHESTNUTS

1 (8½-oz.) can water chestnuts, drained
8 slices bacon, cut in half
¼ cup soy sauce
½ teaspoon ground ginger
½ teaspoon garlic salt

Wrap each water chestnut in half slice of bacon. Secure with toothpick. Combine remaining ingredients. Pour over bacon-wrapped water chestnuts. Refrigerate for several hours. Drain. Marinade can be stored in the refrigerator and reused. Place on metal rack in 7½" x 12" utility dish. Cover with paper towel. Cook on High for 3 minutes. Turn dish. Cook 3 minutes more. Serve hot. Makes 16 appetizers.

OYSTERS-IN-SHELL

1 tablespoon butter
¼ cup water
6 live oysters in shell
¼ cup dry white wine
2 medium garlic cloves, finely chopped

In 2-quart casserole, melt butter with water and bring to boil on High for 1 minute. Arrange oysters evenly in casserole. Add wine and garlic. Cook, covered, on High for 3½ minutes. Let stand, covered, 2 to 3 additional minutes or until shells open slightly. Open and serve on half-shell. Reserve liquid for dipping. Makes 1 to 2 servings.

NACHOS

1 8-oz. pkg. tortilla chips
1½ cups grated Cheddar cheese
1 (4-oz.) can diced green chiles
1 (2¼-oz.) can sliced black olives
Red chile salsa

Empty chips onto serving platter. Cover with Cheddar cheese, then chiles and olives. Sprinkle with chile salsa. Heat for 2 minutes on Low. Makes 4 to 6 servings.
   Variation: Sprinkle 1½ cups grated Monterey Jack jalepeño pepper cheese over chips. Heat on Low for 2 minutes.

COCOA

¼ cup sugar
¼ cup unsweetened powdered cocoa
1 cup water
3 cups milk

In 1½-quart bowl, mix sugar with cocoa. Add water. Heat on High for 1½ minutes, stirring once. Add milk. Heat on High for about 3 minutes or until piping hot, but not boiling. Makes 5 to 6 servings.

HOT WINE-CRANBERRY PUNCH

1 pt. cranberry-juice cocktail
1 cup water
¾ cup sugar
2 sticks cinnamon
6 whole cloves
1 (⅘-qt.) bottle Burgundy wine
1 lemon, sliced

In 3-quart bowl, combine cranberry juice with water, sugar, cinnamon and cloves. Cover. Heat on High for 10 minutes. Strain. Pour strained cranberry mixture back into 3-quart bowl with wine and lemon. Heat on High for 5 minutes or until piping hot. Makes 12 to 15 cups of punch.

MULLED CIDER

1 qt. cider
¼ cup brown sugar, firmly packed
1 stick whole cinnamon
3 whole cloves
   Orange slices

In 2-quart measuring cup or bowl, heat cider with sugar, cinnamon and cloves on High for 6 minutes. Strain and serve hot. Garnish with orange slices. Makes 4 servings.

NEW ENGLAND CLAM CHOWDER

2 slices bacon, diced
1 medium onion, diced
2 medium potatoes, peeled and
    diced
2 (7½-oz.) cans minced clams,
    drained; reserve liquid.
  Add water to make 2 cups liquid.
¼ cup butter, melted
¼ cup unsifted flour
3 cups milk
¾ teaspoon salt
⅛ teaspoon pepper

In 3-quart casserole, cook bacon on High for 3 minutes.
Add onion and potatoes. Cover. Cook on High for 5 minutes. Add clam juice and water. Cover. Cook on High for 8
to 10 minutes or until potatoes are tender. Melt butter in
2-cup liquid measure. Stir in flour and add to potato mixture, mixing well. Add clams and remaining ingredients.
Cover. Cook on High for 4 to 5 minutes or until hot. Makes
4 to 6 servings.

IRISH COUNTRY SOUP

1 (10¾-oz.) can cream-of-potato
    soup
1 (8-oz.) pkg. frozen green peas
    with cream sauce
1 chicken-bouillon cube
2 cups milk

In deep 1½-quart bowl, combine soup, peas, bouillon and milk. Heat on High for 8 to 10 minutes or until bubbly hot, stirring often. Pour into blender. Blend until peas are broken up into small pieces. Makes 4 servings.

OYSTER STEW

4 tablespoons butter
1 pint fresh oysters, drained;
    reserve liquor
1 (13-oz.) can evaporated milk and
    13 oz. water
¼ cup (approximately) oyster liquor
½ teaspoon salt
½ teaspoon pepper
    Chopped chives

In 2-quart casserole, melt butter on High for 45 seconds. Add drained oysters. Cook on High until edges curl, about 4 to 5 minutes. Add milk, water, oyster liquor, salt and pepper. Cook on High 4 minutes longer, or almost to boiling point. Do not let milk boil. Garnish with chives. Makes 4 to 6 servings.

TOMATO CONSOMMÉ

2½ cups tomato juice
1 (10-oz.) can condensed
   consommé
¼ teaspoon seasoned salt
¼ teaspoon crumbled basil
¼ teaspoon sugar
4 lemon slices
8 whole cloves

In 1½-quart bowl, mix tomato juice with consommé, seasoned salt, basil and sugar. Stud lemon slices with cloves. Add to soup. Heat on High for 6 minutes. Makes 4 to 5 servings.

CREAM-OF-CHICKEN SOUP

6 tablespoons butter or margarine
⅓ cup flour
2 cups milk
2 cups chicken broth or bouillon
½ teaspoon seasoned salt
1 cup finely chopped cooked
   chicken

In 2½-quart bowl, melt butter or margarine on High for 45 seconds. Stir in flour, then milk, broth and seasoned salt. Cook on High for 6 minutes, stirring often. Add chicken. Cook 1 minute. Makes 4 to 6 servings.

MINESTRONE SOUP

5 cups hot water
1 lb. beef shanks or stew meat
1 small onion, diced
¼ teaspoon pepper
½ teaspoon basil
½ cup diced carrots
1 (1-lb.) can tomatoes
½ cup uncooked spaghetti, broken
      into 1-inch pieces
2 medium zucchini (3 to 4 inches
      long), sliced
1 (16-oz.) can kidney beans, drained
1 cup shredded cabbage
1 teaspoon salt
   Grated Parmesan or Romano
      cheese

In 4-quart casserole, pour water over meat; add onion,
pepper and basil. Cover. Cook on High for 25 minutes or
until meat is tender, turning meat at least once. Remove
meat from bone and cut into small pieces. Add meat to
soup broth, along with carrots and tomatoes. Cover. Cook
on High for 8 minutes. Stir in spaghetti, zucchini, beans,
cabbage and salt. Cover. Cook on High for another 10 minutes, stirring once. Let stand, covered, several minutes.
Sprinkle with cheese. Makes 6 servings.

SPLIT-PEA SOUP

1 cooked ham shank
1 teaspoon salt
¼ teaspoon pepper
1 small onion, chopped
1 stalk celery, chopped
1 carrot, peeled and chopped
1 lb. dried, split green peas

In 4-quart casserole, cover ham with water. Add salt, pepper, onion, celery, carrot and peas. Cover. Cook on High for 25 minutes. Remove ham shank from casserole; cut off any bits of ham. Add pieces of ham to soup broth. Cover. Cook on High for another 30 minutes or until peas are soft. Thicken with flour, if desired. For smoother consistency, puree soup in blender before serving. Makes 6 to 8 servings.

HOT REUBEN SANDWICHES

2 (3-oz.) pkgs. thin-sliced pressed
     ham or shredded corn beef
2 cups grated Swiss cheese (½ lb.)
1 cup sauerkraut, drained
¾ teaspoon dill weed
½ cup Thousand Island dressing
8 to 12 slices dill-rye or rye bread

In 2½-cup bowl, combine all ingredients, except bread. Toss lightly to mix and coat with dressing. Arrange 4 to 6 slices of bread (depending on size) on a serving platter. Spoon filling generously on each slice. Heat on Medium for 4 to 6 minutes or until cheese starts to melt. Top with remaining slices of bread. Heat on Medium for ½ to 1 minute or until bread is warm. Makes 4 to 6 servings.

BEEF-FILLED SQUASH

2 medium acorn squash
4 slices bacon, diced
¼ cup chopped onion
½ teaspoon salt
1 lb. lean ground beef
½ teaspoon salt
¼ cup fine, dry bread crumbs
1 tablespoon butter or margarine

Cook whole squash on paper towels on High for 8 to 9 minutes or until soft. Let stand for 5 minutes. In 2-quart casserole, cook bacon and onion on High for 3 minutes. Add ½ teaspoon salt and meat. Cook on High for 4 to 5 minutes, stirring often. Cut cooked squash lengthwise; discard seeds and fibers. Carefully remove squash from shells; reserve shells. In small bowl, whip squash with ½ teaspoon salt until squash is fluffy. Combine with the meat mixture. Return to squash shells. Measure bread crumbs into 1-cup measure; add butter or margarine. Heat on High for 1 minute. Stir well. Raise shelf. Cook stuffed shells on Medium for 3 minutes. Top with bread crumb mixture and brown for 5 minutes. Makes 4 servings.

STUFFED FLANK STEAK

¾ cup packaged bread stuffing
1 (3-oz.) can sliced mushrooms, drained
2 tablespoons melted butter or margarine
1 tablespoon grated Parmesan cheese
1 flank steak (about 1¾ lbs.), scored
    on both sides
1 (¾-oz.) pkg. brown-gravy mix
¼ cup dry red wine
2 tablespoons minced green onions
1 tablespoon salad oil
1 garlic clove
¼ cup currant jelly

Combine bread stuffing with mushrooms, butter or margarine and cheese. Spread over flank steak; roll up like jelly roll. Fasten with wooden skewers. Prepare gravy mix according to package directions. Heat on High for 4½ to 5½ minutes, stirring once. Add wine and onions. Pour oil in 7½" x 12" utility dish with garlic clove. Heat on High for 2 minutes. Remove clove. Roll steak in oil, coating all sides. Pour gravy, wine and onions over meat. Cover with plastic wrap. Cook on Low for 35 minutes, turning dish once. Let stand 10 minutes. Remove meat from sauce; add jelly. Heat on High for 2 minutes until jelly is dissolved. Serve sauce over meat. Makes 4 to 6 servings.

SWISS STEAK IN A ROASTING BAG

1½ lbs. thick round steak
¼ cup flour
1 (1-oz.) pkg. seasoning mix for
    Swiss steak
1 (8-oz.) can tomato sauce
½ cup water

Cut steak into serving-size pieces. Coat with flour. Place in single layer in roasting bag. In a 2-cup measure, combine package of seasoning mix, tomato sauce and water. Heat on High for 4 minutes. Pour over steak in bag. Close bag with string or rubber band and place in 7½" x 12" utility dish. Puncture 4 holes in top of bag. Allow to marinate 10 minutes. Cook on Low for 25 minutes. Let stand 10 minutes. Makes 4 to 5 servings.

CHEESE-STUFFED BURGERS

    ¾ cups Basic Creamy-Sauce Mix, pages 213–14
    1¼ cups milk
    1½ cups (6-oz.) grated sharp
        process American cheese
     1 egg, slightly beaten
     1 cup soft bread crumbs
     1 lb. lean ground beef
     1 (3-oz.) can chopped
        mushrooms, drained
     ½ cup cooked rice
     1 tablespoon chopped green onion

In 4-cup measure, combine sauce mix with milk. Cook on High for 2 to 2½ minutes or until thick and bubbly, stirring once. Add cheese and mix until cheese is melted. In medium mixing bowl, combine egg, ⅓ cup of the cooked sauce and bread crumbs. Mix in ground beef. Shape into 4 circles, each circle 6 inches in diameter. Combine ¼ cup of the mushrooms, all of the rice and green onions. Spoon 2 tablespoons of mushroom mixture into center of each meat circle. Fold edges of circles over stuffing and seal. Cook in 7½" x 12" utility dish on High for 5 to 6 minutes, turning burgers over halfway through cooking. Add the rest of the mushrooms to remaining cheese sauce and pour over burgers. Heat on High for 1½ minutes. Spoon sauce over burgers before serving. Makes 4 servings.

BASIC MEATBALLS

3 eggs
½ cup milk
3 cups soft bread crumbs
½ cup finely chopped onion
1 tablespoon oregano
2 teaspoons salt
3 lbs. ground beef

In large mixing bowl, beat eggs. Stir in milk, bread crumbs, onion, oregano and salt. Add meat and mix well. Shape into 72 meatballs 1-inch thick. Arrange in large tray; slip tray in plastic bag and tie. Freeze until firm. Repackage in freezer bags, using 24 meatballs per bag. Tie and freeze. Makes 72 meatballs.

CHINESE MEATBALLS

1½ lbs. ground beef
¾ cup minced celery
½ cup soft bread crumbs
¼ cub chopped almonds
1 large egg
1 tablespoon soy sauce
1 garlic clove, minced
1 teaspoon salt
½ teaspoon MSG
   Sweet-Sour Sauce, page 213

Mix ingredients thoroughly. Form into small meatballs the size of walnuts. Place on the metal meat rack in a 7½" x 12" utility dish, allowing space around each meatball. Cover with paper towel. Cook on High for 5 to 7 minutes. Brown for 6 minutes. Serve with Sweet-Sour Sauce, page 213, as an appetizer or main course. Makes 4 to 6 servings.

TERIYAKI BEEF AND BACON

8 slices bacon
1 lb. lean ground beef
¼ cup soy sauce
2 tablespoons lemon juice
2 tablespoons honey
2 tablespoons white wine
1 garlic clove
¼ teaspoon ground ginger

Place bacon on metal rack in 7½" x 12" utility dish. Cook on High for 2 minutes. Form beef into 4 patties. Wrap each patty in 2 slices of bacon. Secure with toothpicks. Place in shallow dish. Combine remaining ingredients, pour over meat and refrigerate several hours. Drain. Place on metal rack in 7½" x 12" utility dish. Cook on High for 5 to 6 minutes or until done. Raise shelf. Brown for 4 minutes. Makes 4 servings.

MEAT LOAF

TO MAKE 4 SERVINGS:
1 lb. lean ground beef
1 egg
½ cup Italian-seasoned bread crumbs
¼ cup milk
½ cup diced Swiss cheese
2 tablespoons catsup
2 tablespoons dry onion-soup mix
2 tablespoons soy sauce

TO MAKE 6 TO 8 SERVINGS:

2 lbs. lean ground beef
1 egg
1 cup Italian-seasoned bread crumbs
½ cup milk
1 cup diced Swiss cheese
4 tablespoons catsup
3 tablespoons dry onion-soup mix
3 tablespoons soy sauce

Combine all the ingredients and put in a loaf-shaped baking dish, or form by hand into a loaf and place in 2-quart casserole. For a 1-pound meat loaf, cook on Medium for 12 to 14 minutes. For a 2-pound meat loaf, cook on Medium for 20 to 22 minutes. Raise shelf. Brown 5 minutes.

INDIVIDUAL MEAT LOAVES

½ cup soft bread crumbs
½ cup evaporated milk
2 eggs, slightly beaten
1 teaspoon salt
⅛ teaspoon pepper
1 small onion, finely chopped
¼ teaspoon ground thyme
1½ lbs. lean ground beef
¼ lb. process American cheese
¾ cup chili sauce
1 tablespoon Worcestershire sauce
1 teaspoon prepared mustard

In mixing bowl, combine bread crumbs, milk, eggs, salt, pepper, onion and thyme. Add meat; mix well. Cut cheese into 6 cubes. Divide meat into 6 equal portions and form around cheese cubes to make small loaves. Place in 7½" x 12" utility dish. Cover with wax paper. Cook on High for 4 minutes. Turn dish. Cook another 4 minutes. Drain fat. Combine chili sauce, Worcestershire sauce and mustard. Pour over meat. Cook, uncovered, on High for 2 minutes. Makes 6 servings.

BASIC MEAT SAUCE

3 lbs. lean ground beef
2 medium onions, chopped
2 garlic cloves, minced
¾ cup finely chopped celery
1 (28-oz.) can tomatoes, cut up
3 (6-oz.) cans tomato paste
1 cup beef bouillon
2 tablespoons minced parsley
1 tablespoon Worcestershire sauce
1 teaspoon salt
1 teaspoon brown sugar
½ teaspoon pepper
1 bay leaf

In 4-quart casserole, combine beef with onions, garlic and celery. Cover. Cook on High for 10 minutes, stirring twice. Drain excess fat. Add remaining ingredients. Cover. Cook on High for 20 minutes, stirring twice. Add all or part of sauce to main dishes or freeze for future use. Freeze in 1-quart units in freezer cartons or jars. Thaw before using in recipes. Makes about 3 quarts.

MEAT AND POTATO PIE

1 egg, beaten
¾ cup soft bread crumbs
½ cup milk
¼ teaspoon salt
   Dash pepper
1 lb. lean ground beef
½ cup chopped green onion
⅓ cup chili sauce
1 teaspoon prepared mustard
3 cups cooked, diced potatoes
½ cup grated sharp Cheddar cheese

Combine egg, bread crumbs, milk, salt and pepper. Add beef and mix well. Press into bottom and sides of 9-inch pie plate. Cook on High for 3 minutes. Combine onion, chili sauce and mustard. Pour over potatoes and toss lightly. Spoon into baked meat shell. Raise shelf. Cook on High for 3 minutes. Sprinkle with cheese. Brown for 4 minutes. Makes 4 servings.

VEAL SCALOPPINE

1 lb. thin veal cutlets
¼ cup flour
¼ cup butter or margarine
1 garlic clove, minced
4 large fresh mushrooms, sliced
¼ cup dry white wine
1 chicken-bouillon cube
¼ cup hot water
  Salt and pepper

Cut veal into serving-size pieces. Coat with flour. In 7½" x 12" utility dish, melt butter or margarine with garlic on High for 1 minute. Coat meat with butter or margarine mixture. Cook on High for 2 minutes. Stir. Cook on High for another 2 minutes. Add mushrooms, wine and bouillon dissolved in hot water. Cover with wax paper. Cook on High 2 minutes more. Add salt and pepper to taste. Makes 4 servings.

LIVER AND ONIONS

4 slices bacon
1 medium onion, sliced
1 lb. baby-beef liver, sliced
  Salt and pepper

Put bacon on the metal rack in the 7½" x 12" utility dish. Cook on High for 3 to 4 minutes. Cover with paper towel to catch spatters. Remove bacon and metal rack. Set bacon aside to crisp. Add onion slices to bacon drippings in dish; stir to coat. Cook on High for 3 to 4 minutes until light brown, stirring once. Push onions aside. Add liver, coating with drippings. Season with salt and pepper. Put onions on top of liver slices. Crumble bacon and sprinkle on top of onions. Cover with wax paper. Cook on High for 2½ to 3½ minutes until pink color is barely gone. Turn dish and re-arrange liver slices once. Brown as desired. Makes 4 servings.

FREEZER-TO-TABLE POT ROAST

1 (3-lb.) beef chuck roast,
    completely frozen
1 (1¼ to 1½ oz.) envelope dry
    onion-soup mix
1 lb. (4 small) new potatoes, peeled
    and quartered
1 cup sliced celery, cut 1-inch thick
2 cups slivered carrots, cut
    2-inches long

Place completely frozen meat in 3-quart casserole. Cover tightly. Cook on Low for 30 minutes. Turn over and sprinkle with ½ the onion-soup mix. Cover. Cook on Low for an additional 30 minutes. Turn meat over again and sprinkle with remaining onion-soup mix. Add vegetables around meat with onion rings on top. Cover. Cook on Low for 20 to 30 minutes until meat and vegetables are tender. Let stand, covered, 10 minutes. Makes 4 to 6 servings.

MINTED LAMB CHOPS

½ cup wine vinegar
½ cup apple-mint jelly
2 tablespoons brown sugar
1 tablespoon lemon juice
1 teaspoon grated lemon peel
½ teaspoon dry mustard
6 loin lamb chops (about 2 lbs.),
      1-inch thick
   Salt and pepper

In 4-cup measure, combine vinegar, jelly, sugar, lemon juice, lemon peel and mustard. Heat on High for 2 minutes or until jelly melts, stirring once. Cool slightly; pour over lamb chops. Marinate several hours. Drain and reserve marinade. Place lamb chops on metal rack in 7½" x 12" utility dish. Brush with marinade. Raise shelf. Cook on High for 4 minutes. Turn chops and brush with marinade. Raise shelf. Cook on High for 4 minutes. Sprinkle with salt and pepper. Brown 5 minutes. Makes 3 servings.

LEMON-BUTTER GLAZED LAMB ROAST

1 (5-lb.) lamb roast, boned
   Freshly ground pepper
1 teaspoon ground oregano
3 garlic cloves
¼ cup butter
⅓ cup lemon juice
1 teaspoon soy sauce

Sprinkle all sides of lamb with pepper and oregano. Cut 1 garlic clove and rub over roast. Crush remaining garlic. In 1-cup measure melt butter on High for 40 seconds. Add lemon juice, soy sauce and remaining garlic. Place roast, skin side down, on metal rack in 7½" x 12" utility dish. Pour half the glaze over meat. Cook on Medium for 12 minutes.

Turn dish. Cook a second 12 minutes. Turn roast over. Protect edges and small end from overcooking with small pieces of foil. Pour remaining glaze over meat. Cook on Medium for a final 12 minutes. Turn dish. Cook 14 minutes. Brown 4 to 5 minutes. Remove from oven. Cover with foil and let stand 20 minutes. Makes about 6 servings.

GLAZED PORK ROAST

1 tablespoon cornstarch
1 tablespoon lemon juice
1 (8-oz.) can crushed pineapple,
    not drained
1 cup apricot nectar
2 tablespoons soy sauce
1 tablespoon corn syrup
4–lb. pork-loin roast, boned
    Salt and pepper

In 4-cup measure, dissolve cornstarch in lemon juice. Stir in undrained pineapple, apricot nectar, soy sauce and corn syrup. Cook on High for 4 minutes, stirring twice. Set aside. Place roast, fat side down, on metal rack in 7½" x 12" utility dish. Brush with sauce and cover with wax paper. Cook on Medium for 9 minutes. Give dish a half turn. Cook for a second 9 minutes. Turn roast fat side up and brush with sauce. Cook on Medium for a third 9 minutes. Sprinkle with salt and pepper. Give dish a half turn again. Cook on Medium for a final 9 minutes. Brush with sauce. Brown 5 minutes. Let stand 10 minutes before carving. Serve with extra sauce. Makes 4 to 6 servings.

PORK HAWAIIAN

3 cups cubed cooked pork (about
    1½ lbs.)
⅓ cup brown sugar, firmly packed
2 tablespoons cornstarch
½ teaspoon ground ginger
¼ teaspoon garlic powder
¼ cup soy sauce
2 tablespoons catsup
1 onion, cut in chunks
1 green pepper, cubed
1 (20-oz.) can pineapple chunks
    packed in pineapple juice
⅓ cup wine vinegar
¼ cup soy sauce
1 tablespoon cornstarch
1 (8-oz.) can water chestnuts,
    drained
1 (3-oz.) jar sliced mushrooms

Place pork cubes in a 2½-quart glass-ceramic casserole. Combine brown sugar, cornstarch, ginger and garlic powder in a 2-cup liquid measure. Stir in soy sauce and catsup. Pour over pork. Stir to coat all of pork. Cook on High for 3 minutes. Add onion and green pepper. Cook on High for 4 minutes. Drain pineapple, reserving juice. To pineapple juice add water to make 1 cup of liquid. Add vinegar and soy sauce. Stir in cornstarch. Pour over cooked pork. Cook on High for 6 to 7 minutes until sauce is thick. Add water chestnuts and pineapple chunks. Continue to cook on High for 2 to 3 minutes. Serve over hot rice. Makes 6 to 8 servings.

CALICO STUFFED PEPPERS

3 large green peppers
1 lb. bulk sausage
¾ cup chopped onion
1 (8-oz.) can whole-kernel corn, drained
3 tablespoons catsup
¼ teaspoon garlic salt
1 (8-oz.) can tomato sauce
½ cup grated Cheddar cheese

Wash peppers and cut in half lengthwise. Cut stems; scoop out seeds. In covered 4-quart casserole, cook peppers on High for 4 minutes. In 2-quart casserole, cook sausage and onion on High for 5 minutes, stirring once. Drain excess fat. Stir in corn, catsup and garlic salt. Spoon mixture into peppers. Return stuffed peppers to 4-quart casserole. Pour tomato sauce over all. Cover. Cook on High for 5 minutes. Sprinkle with cheese. Cook, uncovered, for 1 additional minute. Makes 6 servings.

ORIENTAL HAM KABOBS

1 green pepper
1 (14-oz.) can pineapple chunks,
     drained; reserve ¼ cup syrup
1 lb. cooked ham, cut into 1-inch cubes

Plum Sauce:
1 (1 lb.) can purple plums, drained
¾ cup sugar
2 tablespoons cornstarch
⅓ cup vinegar
¼ cup pineapple syrup from canned pineapple
2 teaspoons dry minced onion
½ teaspoon salt

Wash pepper and cut in half lengthwise. Cut stem; scoop out seeds. Place on paper towel and partially cook on High for 1½ minutes. Cube. Drain pineapple chunks, reserving syrup. Thread ham, pineapple and green pepper on wooden skewers. Brush kabobs with plum sauce. Raise shelf. Cook on High for 2 minutes. Brown for 3½ minutes. Turn kabobs over. Brush with more sauce. Brown for 3 to 4 minutes. Makes 4 servings.

Plum Sauce: Pit plums and puree in blender. Blend sugar with cornstarch. In 4-cup measure, add to vinegar, pineapple juice, onion and salt. Cook on High for 5 minutes, stirring twice. Mix in pureed plums.

BAVARIAN PORK CHOPS

1 (1-lb.) can sauerkraut, drained
¼ teaspoon caraway seeds
1 cooking apple, cored, peeled and grated
4 loin or rib pork chops (1½ to 2 lbs.)
  Salt and pepper

In bottom of 7½" x 12" utility dish, combine sauerkraut with caraway seeds and apple. Top with pork chops. Cover with wax paper. Cook on Medium for 4 to 5 minutes and turn chops. Cook another 4 to 5 minutes. Sprinkle with salt and pepper. Makes 6 servings.

OVEN-BAKED CHICKEN

1 (3-lb.) fryer, cut up
1 pkg. seasoned coating mix for chicken

Coat chicken with seasoned coating mix, according to directions on package. Place chicken in 7½" x 12" utility dish, skin side down, with the meaty pieces to the outside of the dish. Cover with paper towel. Raise shelf. Cook on High for 10 minutes. Turn dish. Cook for 10 to 11 minutes more. Brown 6 minutes. Makes 4 servings.

ROAST CHICKEN WITH STUFFING & PAN GRAVY

1 (4-lb.) roasting chicken
1 (6½-oz.) pkg. stuffing mix
  Salad oil

Pan Gravy:
½ cup pan drippings
¼ cup flour
1½ cup hot water or bouillon
  Salt and pepper

Rinse chicken; pat dry. Prepare stuffing mix according to package directions. Stuff bird. Tie legs together; tuck wings under. Place, breast side down, on metal rack 7½" x 12" utility dish. Brush with oil. Cook on Medium for 10 minutes. Turn dish. Cook for second 10 minutes. Turn breast side up and baste with drippings. Cook on Medium for a third 10 minutes. Turn dish. Cook for a final 10 minutes. Brown for 6 minutes. After browning, remove from dish, cover and let stand for 5 minutes. Serve with pan gravy. Makes 6 servings.

Pan Gravy: Reserve ½ cup pan drippings. Stir in flour to make a smooth paste. Cook on High for 3 minutes, stirring twice. Add hot water or bouillon. Cook on High for 3 to 4 minutes or until thickened. Add salt and pepper to taste. Makes 2 cups.

CHICKEN PARMESAN

1 cut-up chicken
⅓ cup butter or margarine
1½ cups Parmesan cheese
3 teaspoons paprika
2 teaspoons salt
1 teaspoon pepper

In 7½" x 12" utility dish, melt butter or margarine on High for 40 seconds. Coat chicken with butter. Combine rest of the ingredients in a bag and add pieces of chicken one at a time. Shake to coat with crumb mixture. Place skin side down in the dish with the thickest pieces to the outer edge. Cover with paper towel to absorb any spatter. Cook on Medium, 10 minutes per pound. After half of the cooking time, turn chicken pieces over, skin side up. Sprinkle with remaining crumb mixture. Finish cooking on Medium. Brown as desired. Makes 4 servings.

CREAMED CHICKEN

1 pkg. frozen green peas with
   cream sauce
¾ cup milk
1 tablespoon butter or margarine
   Curry powder to taste
1 cup diced, cooked chicken

Put frozen peas, milk and butter or margarine in 2-quart casserole. Cover. Cook on High for 5 minutes. Remove from oven. Add the curry powder and stir until smooth. Fold in chicken. Cook on High for 1 to 2 minutes or until hot. Serve over rice. Makes 2 servings.

DEACON'S HOT CURRIED-CHICKEN SALAD

1 barbecued chicken, skinned and
   diced
1¼ cups chopped celery
1 small jar chopped pimientos
1 small green pepper, chopped
1 small onion, chopped
3 hard-cooked eggs, chopped
⅓ cup cashew nuts, coarsely
   chopped

1¼ cups mayonnaise
 ½ teaspoon salt
 ¼ teaspoon pepper
 ¼ teaspoon celery salt
   Curry powder to taste
 4 tablespoons lemon juice
 1 cup chopped Cheddar cheese
1½ cups crushed potato chips

In 7½" x 12" utility dish, mix all the ingredients together, except the Cheddar cheese and potato chips. Raise shelf. Cook on High for 3 minutes. Stir. Cook for 2 minutes. Sprinkle with the Cheddar cheese. Cook for 1 minute. Sprinkle with potato chips. Brown 4 to 5 minutes. Makes 4 servings.

CHICKEN MARENGO

2½ lbs. chicken parts
 ¼ cup flour
 ¼ cup salad oil
 1 (1½-oz.) pkg. spaghetti-sauce
     mix
 ½ cup dry white wine
 3 tomatoes, quartered
 ¼ lb. fresh mushrooms, halved

Rinse chicken and pat dry. Coat with flour and roll in oil. Place skin side up in 7½" x 12" utility dish, with meaty pieces to the outside of the dish. Cover with wax paper. Cook on High for 8 minutes. Combine dry spaghetti-sauce mix, wine and tomatoes. Pour over chicken. Cover. Cook on High for 8 additional minutes. Add mushrooms. Cover. Cook on High for 1 minute. Makes 4 to 5 servings.

CHICKEN 'N RICE

3 tablespoons butter or margarine
2 to 2½ lbs. chicken parts
½ lb. brown-and-serve sausages, cut
    into chunks
1 (16-oz.) can stewed tomatoes
1 cup chicken bouillon
½ teaspoon salt
1 cup uncooked rice

In 4-quart casserole, melt butter or margarine on High for 35 seconds. Coat chicken parts with melted butter or margarine. Cover. Cook on High for 8 minutes. Combine remaining ingredients. Spoon over chicken. Cover. Cook on High for 15 minutes or until rice is cooked. Let stand, covered for 10 minutes before serving. Makes 4 to 5 servings.

CHICKEN IN THE BAG

1 (2½ to 3-lb.) frying chicken, cut up
1 (1⅜-oz.) oven cooking bag with
    coating mix for chicken
1 (4-oz.) can mushrooms
   Water
2 onions, quartered
½ cup catsup

Wash chicken; dry with paper towels. Place chicken in cooking bag, skin side up. Drain mushrooms; save liquid. Add water to make ½ cup. Arrange onions around chicken. Blend coating mix with the mushroom liquid and catsup. Pour sauce mixture over chicken. Close bag with rubber band or string. Place bag in 7½" x 12" utility dish. Punch 4 small holes along top of bag. Cook on High for 10 minutes; turn dish. Cook for 10 minutes more. Add mushrooms and let stand for 10 minutes. Makes 4 to 5 servings.

SHERRIED CHICKEN BAKE

2 full chicken breasts, (approximately 1½ lbs.),
     skinned, boned, and halved lengthwise
1 cup cocktail sherry
1 small box dry coating mix for chicken
1 teaspoon thyme
½ teaspoon paprika
¼ cup butter or margarine

Let chicken marinate in sherry for 3 minutes. In small bag,
blend dry chicken coating mix with thyme and paprika.
Coat chicken with mixture. In 7½" x 12" utility dish, melt the
butter or margarine on High for 40 seconds. Add chicken,
coating both sides with melted butter or margarine. Place
thick side of breast to the outer edge of the dish. Cover dish
with plastic wrap. Cook on Medium for 7 minutes. Turn
chicken over and rearrange in the dish. Cover dish with the
plastic wrap. Cook 7 minutes more on Medium. Brown 6 to
8 minutes, if desired. Makes 4 servings.

VARIATION: Serve on rice with Sherry-Mushroom Sauce.

SHERRY-MUSHROOM SAUCE

1 (1-oz.) pkg. chicken-gravy mix
½ cup sliced fresh mushrooms
1 cup cocktail sherry that the
     chicken marinated in
1 cup dairy sour cream, room
     temperature

After chicken has cooked, remove from dish. Add chicken-
gravy mix to the drippings. Stir well. Cook on High for 4
minutes. Add mushrooms and sherry. Cook on High for 2
minutes. Stir in sour cream. Heat on High for 1 minute. If
desired, thin with additional sherry or water.

CHICKEN DIJON

3 tablespoons butter or margarine
4 chicken breasts (about 2 lbs.), boned,
      skinned and halved lengthwise
2 tablespoons all-purpose flour
1 cup chicken broth
½ cup light cream
2 tablespoons Dijon-style mustard

In 7½" x 12" utility dish, melt the butter or margarine on High for 35 seconds. Coat chicken on both sides with melted butter or margarine. Cover. Cook on High for 6 minutes. Turn dish. Cook on High for an additional 6 minutes. Place chicken on warm platter and set aside. Stir flour into drippings. Add broth and cream. Cook on High, stirring often, until mixture is thick. Stir in mustard. Pour sauce over chicken. Heat on High for 1½ minutes. Makes 4 servings.

CHICKEN BREASTS, FRENCH STYLE

3 large chicken breasts (about 3 lbs.),
      boned, skinned and halved lengthwise
6 slices Prosciutto or thinly sliced ham
6 thin slices Swiss or American cheese
      Pepper
2 tablespoons butter or margarine
1 (10¾-oz.) can cream-of-mushroom soup
2 tablespoons dry white wine
1 (3-oz.) can sliced mushrooms, drained

Pound chicken breasts with wooden mallet until about ¼-inch thick. Place 1 slice of ham and cheese on each. Tuck in sides and roll up as for jelly roll. Skewer with toothpick or tie securely. Sprinkle with pepper. Melt butter or margarine in 7½" x 12" utility dish on High for 30 seconds. Coat chicken with melted butter or margarine. Cook on High for 10 minutes. Combine soup with wine and add mushrooms, if desired. Pour over chicken. Cover with wax paper. Cook on High for 10 to 11 minutes, turning dish once. Let stand 8 to 10 minutes before serving. Makes 6 servings.

HAWAIIAN FRIED CHICKEN

¼ cup soy sauce
¼ cup white wine
  Juice of 1 lime
1 garlic clove, minced
¼ teaspoon ground ginger
¼ teaspoon oregano
¼ teaspoon thyme
3 whole chicken breasts (about 3 lbs.), halved
¼ cup flour
½ cup butter or margarine

Combine soy sauce with wine, lime juice, garlic, ginger, oregano and thyme. Pour over chicken. Marinate for several hours, turning 2 or 3 times. Drain sauce. Pat chicken dry with paper towels. Coat with flour. In 7½" x 12" utility dish, melt butter or margarine on High for 1 minute. Add chicken, skin side down. Raise shelf. Cook on High for 9 to 10 minutes. Turn chicken; brush with butter. Cook on High for 9 to 10 minutes. Brown for 6 to 8 minutes. Makes 6 servings.

COUNTRY-STYLE CHICKEN

1 (3-lb.) frying chicken, cut up
  Seasoned flour
¼ cup butter or margarine

Coat chicken with seasoned flour. Melt butter or margarine in 7½" x 12" utility dish on High for 40 seconds. Roll chicken in melted butter or margarine. Place, skin side down, in utility dish with the meaty pieces to the outside. Cover with wax paper. Raise shelf. Cook on Medium for 15 minutes. Turn chicken over. Cook for 15 minutes more. Remove wax paper. Brown for 8 minutes. Let stand for 5 minutes. Makes 4 to 5 servings.

CHINESE-GLAZED CORNISH HEN

2 Cornish hens, 15 to 18 oz. each
1 recipe Chinese Rice Stuffing, below
1 recipe Chinese Apricot Glaze, page 166
¼ cup butter, melted

Thoroughly defrost Cornish hens as described in table, page 99. Remove giblets, rinse and dry. Stuff each hen with half of Chinese Rice Stuffing, close mouth of cavity securely with toothpicks. Tie legs of each hen together with string, then cover ends of legs with a small piece of foil (one piece of foil covering both legs). Place hens, breast side down, on wire rack in 7½" x 12" utility dish. Brush with butter. Cook on Medium for 15 minutes. Turn hens breast side up. Brush with butter. Cook on Medium for 5 minutes. Brush a generous coating of Chinese Apricot Glaze on each hen. Continue to cook on Medium for 12 to 15 minutes, brushing twice with glaze until done. Let stand 10 minutes before serving. Makes 2 to 4 servings.

CHINESE RICE STUFFING

¼ cup butter
2 tablespoons minced onion
4 medium mushrooms, chopped
¼ cup chopped dried apricots
1 tablespoon chopped dried parsley
⅛ teaspoon ginger
1½ teaspoons soy sauce
1½ cups cooked white or brown rice

In 1-quart casserole, combine butter, onion and mushrooms. Cover. Cook on High for 2 to 3 minutes or until vegetables are tender. Stir in remaining ingredients. Use to stuff 2 Cornish hens or 1 chicken. Makes about 1¼ cups of stuffing.

CHINESE APRICOT GLAZE

½ cup dried apricots
¾ cup water
1½ teaspoons grated orange peel
¼ cup orange juice
3 tablespoons dark corn syrup
1 tablespoon cider vinegar
1 tablespoon soy sauce
½ teaspoon ground ginger

In 2-cup liquid measure, combine apricots and water. Cook on High for 3 to 4 minutes or until mixture boils. Turn to Low and continue cooking for 3 to 5 minutes or until apricots are soft and plump. Let stand a few minutes. Drain. Combine apricots and remaining ingredients in a blender container. Blend on low speed until smooth. Use to baste Cornish hens. Also good on chicken. Makes about 1¼ cups of glaze.

ROAST TURKEY WITH COUNTRY GRAVY

1 (10-lb.) turkey
  Salt
2 stalks celery, chopped
1 small onion, chopped
¼ cup butter or margarine
1 (7-oz.) pkg. poultry dressing
¾ cup water
½ cup oil
½ teaspoon brown sauce for gravy

Country Gravy:
1 cup pan drippings
½ cup flour
2 cups hot water, consommé or beef stock
  Salt and pepper

Wash turkey; pat dry with paper towel. Sprinkle inside with salt. In 4-cup measure, combine celery and onion with butter or margarine. Cook on High for 5 minutes. Add to package dressing with water. Spoon into cavities of turkey. Tie legs together, then to tail. Close neck cavity with small wooden skewer. Tie string around center of turkey to hold wings against body. Combine oil and brown sauce for gravy. Brush bird with oil mixture. Place, breast side down, on metal rack in 7½" x 12" utility dish. Place wax paper over bird. Allow 9½ to 10½ minutes per pound on Medium for total cooking time. Cook ¼ of the total time, turn dish and baste with oil mixture. Cook ¼ of the time, turn turkey, breast side up, and baste. Cook ¼ of the time, turn dish again and baste. Cook the final ¼ length of time. Remove from dish and cover with foil for 20 minutes. Serve with Country Gravy. Makes 8 servings.

Country Gravy: Reserve 1 cup drippings in the utility dish. Stir in flour to make a smooth paste. Cook on High for 8 minutes, stirring twice. Add hot liquid and cook on High for 5 minutes more. Add salt and pepper to taste. Makes 3 cups.

CHICKEN-NOODLE CASSEROLE

4 oz. noodles, cooked and drained
1 (10¾-oz.) can cream-of-mushroom soup
¾ cup milk
¼ lb. mild Cheddar cheese, grated (1 cup)
⅓ cup chopped green pepper
2 tablespoons chopped pimiento
½ teaspoon salt
¼ teaspoon pepper
2 cups cooked, diced chicken
¾ cup crushed potato chips

On cooktop, cook noodles according to package directions. Drain. Combine noodles with remaining ingredients, except potato chips, in a 2½-quart casserole. Mix well. Cover. Cook on High for 10 minutes, stirring after half the cooking time. Stir. Sprinkle with potato chips. Brown 5 to 6 minutes or as desired. Makes 6 servings.

CRANBERRY-GLAZED TURKEY ROAST

1 (3-lb.) frozen, boneless, rolled turkey roast
1 (8-oz.) can whole-berry cranberry sauce
2 tablespoons orange marmalade
2 tablespoons red wine
¼ teaspoon cinnamon
  Melted butter or margarine

Thaw roast for 5 minutes per pound on Low. Let stand for 10 minutes halfway through thawing. Turn roast over halfway through thawing. In 4-cup measure, heat cranberry sauce, marmalade, wine and cinnamon on High for 2 minutes; set aside. Cut plastic bag from turkey, but do not remove net. Brush with melted butter or margarine. Place turkey on metal rack in 7½" x 12" utility dish. Cover with wax paper. Cook on Medium for 11 minutes. Turn roast over and brush with cranberry glaze. Cook for a second 11 minutes. Turn dish and brush roast with glaze. Cook on Medium for a third 11 minutes. Remove wax paper. Brown 6 minutes. Remove roast from oven and cover with foil for 5 minutes. Serve with remaining sauce. Makes 6 servings.

CHICKEN CORDON BLEU

4 whole chicken breasts (about
    4 lbs.) boned with all the skin
    possible intact
4 slices Prosciutto or Westphalian ham
4 thin slices Muenster or Monterey Jack cheese
2 tablespoon butter or margarine

Mushroom-Cheese Sauce:

2 tablespoons flour
  Drippings from cooked chicken breasts
1 cup grated Cheddar or Monterey Jack cheese
¼ cup milk
¼ cup white wine
½ cup sliced fresh mushrooms
¼ cup sliced green onion

Pound each breast to ¼-inch thick. Place ½ slice of ham and cheese on each breast half. Be sure that cheese does not come near the edge of the chicken. Fold the sides together, pinning through the skin with round toothpicks. In 7½" x 12" utility dish, melt 2 tablespoons butter or margarine on High for 30 seconds. Coat the chicken in the hot butter or margarine. Place the thick side of the breast towards the outside of the dish. Cover with wax paper. Raise shelf. Cook on Medium for 20 minutes. Turn chicken over, thick side towards the outside of the dish. Cover. Cook 20 minutes more on Medium. Uncover. Brown 5 to 6 minutes. Reserve drippings. Serve with Mushroom-Cheese Sauce. Makes 4 servings.

Sauce: Stir flour into drippings and make a smooth paste. Add cheese and mix well. Add milk and wine and stir. Cook on High for 3 to 4 minutes or until mixture comes to medium boil. Add mushrooms. Cook on High for 1½ to 2 minutes. Pour sauce over the Cordon Bleu. Garnish with green onions.

MARY'S CHICKEN DIVAN

2 (10-oz.) pkgs. frozen broccoli spears
2 whole chicken breasts (about 2 lbs.),
    boned, skinned and halved
2 (10¾-oz.) cans condensed cream-of-mushroom soup
1 cup mayonnaise
1 teaspoon lemon juice

½ teaspoon curry powder (optional)
½ cup shredded sharp Cheddar cheese
½ cup soft bread crumbs
2 tablespoons butter or margarine

Pierce packages and partially thaw the broccoli in the packages on High for 4½ minutes. Place chicken in 7½" x 12" utility dish. Cover with wax paper. Cook on High for 7 minutes. Remove chicken and slice. Arrange broccoli spears in the utility dish. Place sliced chicken over the broccoli. Combine soup, mayonnaise, lemon juice and curry powder, if desired. Pour over the chicken. Cover with plastic wrap. Raise shelf. Cook on High for 5 minutes. Remove plastic wrap and sprinkle the cheese on top of the casserole. Measure bread crumbs into a 1-cup measure and add butter or margarine. Heat on High for 1 minute. Mix well. Top casserole with bread crumbs. Brown for 4 minutes. Makes 4 servings.

FISH AND SEAFOOD

LOBSTER THERMIDOR

⅓ cup butter
½ cup sifted flour
3 cups half and half, room temperature
2 tablespoons white wine
¼ teaspoon dry mustard
   Pinch of cayenne pepper
¼ cup butter
½ lb. fresh mushrooms, sliced
3 cups cooked lobster meat, cut in 1-inch pieces
¼ cup grated Parmesan cheese
1½ teaspoons salt
   Parmesan cheese

In 4-quart casserole, melt ⅓ cup butter on High in 40 seconds. Stir in flour to make a paste. Add half and half gradually. Cook sauce on Medium for 13 minutes, stirring occasionally. Add wine, mustard and cayenne to sauce and set aside. Melt ¼ cup butter in a 2-quart casserole on High for 40 seconds. Add mushrooms and sauté on High for 4 minutes. Add mushroom mixture to sauce along with lobster, ¼ cup cheese and salt. Heat on High for 5 minutes. Sprinkle Parmesan cheese over top. Brown for 5 minutes. Serve over cooked rice. Makes 4 servings.

SEAFOOD NEWBURG

2 tablespoons butter or margarine
2 tablespoons flour
1½ cups light cream
2 tablespoons dry white wine
1 cup sliced fresh mushrooms
½ teaspoon salt
⅛ teaspoon onion salt
⅛ teaspoon pepper
 Dash nutmeg
2 egg yolks
1 cup cooked lobster tails, cut into
 small chunks
1 cup cooked crab meat or shrimp
 Chopped chives

In 2-quart casserole, melt butter or margarine on High for 30 seconds. Stir in flour to make a smooth paste. Add cream, wine, mushrooms and seasonings. Cook on High for 5 to 6 minutes, stirring often. Beat egg yolks. Stir part of sauce into yolks. Then return egg-yolk mixture to casserole. Cook on Medium for 2 minutes, stirring every 15 seconds. Stir in seafood. Cook on High for 1 minute or until hot. Sprinkle with chives. Serve in baked patty shells or toast cups. Makes 4 to 5 servings.

SALMON NEWBURG

½ cup Basic Creamy-Sauce Mix, page 213–14
1 cup light cream
½ cup water
3 egg yolks, slightly beaten
3 tablespoons dry white wine
2 teaspoons lemon juice
¼ teaspoon salt
¼ teaspoon dried tarragon, crushed
1 (16-oz.) can salmon, drained and
    bones removed, broken into chunks
4 frozen patty shells, baked

In 2-quart casserole, combine sauce mix, cream and water.
Cook on High for 2 minutes until thickened and bubbly,
stirring often. Stir small amount of hot mixture into egg
yolks. Return egg-yolk mixture to casserole. Cook on High
for about 1 minute or until thick, stirring often. Stir in
wine, lemon juice, salt and tarragon. Add salmon chunks.
Cook on High for 2 minutes or until hot. Spoon into baked
patty shells. Makes 4 servings.

SCALLOPED OYSTERS

½ cup butter
2 cups coarse cracker crumbs
    (40 saltine crackers)
½ teaspoon salt
⅛ teaspoon pepper
½ teaspoon Worcestershire sauce
¼ cup minced celery
1 pint oysters, drained; reserve liquor
¼ cup (approximately) oyster liquor,
    plus milk to equal ¾ cup
Minced parsley

Melt butter on High for 45 seconds. Combine with cracker crumbs, salt, pepper, Worcestershire sauce and celery. Spread ⅓ of mixture in a 2-quart buttered casserole. Layer ½ oysters over crumb mixture. Repeat layers, leaving top with leftover crumb mixture. Pour oyster liquor and milk mixture over contents of dish. Cook on High for 15 minutes, rotating ¼ turn halfway through cooking time. Let stand 5 minutes. Garnish with parsley. Makes 6 servings.

POACHED SALMON STEAKS

1½ cups hot water
 ⅓ cup dry white wine
 2 peppercorns
 1 lemon, thinly sliced
 1 bay leaf
 1 tablespoon instant minced onion
 1 teaspoon seasoned salt
 4 or 5 salmon steaks

Sauce:
 ½ cup dairy sour cream
 1 tablespoon minced parsley
 1 teaspoon lemon juice
 ½ teaspoon dried dill weed

In 7½" x 12" utility dish, combine all ingredients except salmon and heat on High for 5 minutes or until boiling. Carefully place fish in hot liquid. Cover with plastic wrap. Cook on High for 2 minutes. Let stand 5 minutes. Drain. Serve with sauce. Makes 4 to 5 servings.

Sauce: Combine sauce ingredients. Serve with salmon.

TUNA PATTIES

2 eggs, slightly beaten
1 cup soft bread crumbs
1 tablespoon pickle relish
2 teaspoons instant minced onion
2 teaspoons lemon juice
½ teaspoon Worcestershire sauce
2 (6½-oz.) cans tuna, drained and flaked
2 tablespoons butter or margarine
1 (8-oz.) pkg. frozen peas with cream sauce
   Milk
   Butter
2 hard-cooked eggs

In bowl, combine eggs with bread crumbs, relish, onion, lemon juice and Worcestershire sauce. Add tuna; mix thoroughly. Shape into 4 patties about 1-inch thick. Raise shelf. In 7½" x 12" utility dish, melt butter on High for 30 seconds. Arrange patties in dish with butter. Cover with wax paper. Cook on High for 8 minutes. Turn patties over. Cover. Cook 2 minutes more on High. Uncover and brown 5 minutes. Put frozen peas in a 4-cup measure and combine with amount of milk and butter as indicated on package of peas. Cook on High for 4 minutes, stirring once. Peel and chop eggs; add to sauce. Pour over cooked tuna patties. Makes 4 servings.

SOLE VERONIQUE

1 lb. fillet of sole
1 cup sauterne wine
¼ cup butter or margarine
1 tablespoon cornstarch
⅔ cup light cream
½ teaspoon salt
1 cup seedless grapes

Cut fish into serving-size portions. In 7½" x 12" utility dish, pour ⅔ cups wine over fish. Reserve ⅓ cup wine. Cover with plastic wrap. Cook on High 4 to 5 minutes, turning dish once. Drain fillets. In 4-cup measure, melt butter or margarine on High for 40 seconds. Dissolve cornstarch in cream. Add salt and stir into melted butter or margarine. Add ⅓ cup reserved wine to cream mixture. Cook on High for 1 minute, stirring once. Cook on Medium for 2 to 2½ minutes, stirring every 30 seconds to prevent sauce from curdling. Add grapes. Place cooked sole in platter suitable for use in microwave. Pour sauce with grapes over fish. Cook on High for 30 seconds. Makes 3 to 4 servings.

TUNA TETRAZZINI

¼ cup butter or margarine
¼ cup flour
1 cup light cream
1 cup chicken bouillon
2 tablespoons white wine
½ teaspoon seasoned salt
½ cup grated Cheddar cheese
¼ cup sliced green onions
1 (2-oz.) can sliced mushrooms,
    drained
2 (6½-oz.) can tuna, drained
2 cups cooked thin spaghetti
¼ cup fresh-chopped parsley

In 7½" x 12" utility dish, melt butter and margarine on High for 40 seconds. Stir in flour, then cream, bouillon, wine and seasoned salt. Cook on High for 5 minutes, stirring twice. Fold in Cheddar cheese, green onions, mushrooms, tuna and drained spaghetti. Cover with wax paper. Cook on High for 3 to 4 minutes. Garnish with chopped parsley. Makes 4 to 5 servings.

SHRIMP CURRY

1 cup diced celery
½ cup chopped onion
¼ cup butter
5 tablespoons flour
1 teaspoon salt
1 teaspoon curry powder
½ teaspoon sugar
⅛ teaspoon ginger
2 chicken-bouillon cubes
2 cups hot water
1 lb. cooked shrimp, drained
½ teaspoon lemon juice
2 tablespoons sherry

In 1½-quart casserole, combine celery, onion, and butter. Cover. Cook on High for 6 to 7 minutes, until onions and celery are limp. Stir in flour, salt, curry powder, sugar and ginger. Cover. Cook on High for 1 minute. Dissolve bouillon cubes in water. Gradually add bouillon to flour mixture, stirring until smooth. Cover. Cook on High for 5 to 7 minutes until thickened and smooth, stirring occasionally. Add shrimp and lemon juice. Cover. Heat on High for 2 to 3 minutes to heat shrimp. Stir in sherry. Serve over hot rice with condiments. Makes 4 to 6 servings.

Condiments: Chopped peanuts, coconut, chopped hard-cooked egg, crisp crumbled bacon, chutney, raisins.

BARBECUED HALIBUT STEAKS

4 halibut steaks (about 2-lbs.), 1-inch thick
¼ cup catsup
2 tablespoons salad oil
2 tablespoons lemon juice
1 teaspoon Worcestershire sauce
½ teaspoon prepared mustard
¼ teaspoon garlic salt
   Several drops liquid smoke

Arrange halibut steaks in 7½" x 12" utility dish or serving platter. Combine remaining ingredients. Brush fish with sauce and cover with wax paper. Raise shelf. Cook on High for 3 minutes. Brush with sauce. Cook another 3 to 5 minutes. Brown 5 minutes. Makes 4 servings.

FILLETS AMANDINE

¼ cup slivered, blanched almonds
2 tablespoons butter or margarine
3 tablespoons butter or margarine
2 tablespoons lemon juice
1½ lbs. fish fillets, cut into individual portions
½ teaspoon salt

In 2-cup measure, combine almonds and 2 tablespoons butter or margarine. Cook on High 2 to 3 minutes or until golden brown. In 7½" x 12" utility dish, melt 3 tablespoons butter or margarine on High for 35 seconds. Stir in lemon juice and add fish. Cover with wax paper. Cook on High for 2 minutes. Turn dish and cook 3 minutes (depending on thickness of fillets). Sprinkle with salt and buttered almonds. Makes 2 servings.

LEMON-BUTTER-DRENCHED SCAMPI

1 lb. large, raw shrimp
¼ cup butter or margarine
1 garlic clove, minced
2 tablespoons lemon juice
1 tablespoon minced parsley
½ teaspoon salt
⅛ teaspoon pepper

Peel shrimp, clean and remove vein. Split along back curve, cutting deep, almost to edge. Open, then press flat, butterfly-style. In 7½" x 12" utility dish, melt butter or margarine on High for 40 seconds. Add the remaining ingredients. Stir well to coat shrimp. Cook on High for 1 minute. Stir. Cook another 1½ to 2 minutes. Serve immediately. Makes 2 servings.

ONE-DISH MEALS

SPANISH STUFFED ONIONS

4 large onions, peeled (about 1½ lbs.)
¼ cup water
½ lb. lean ground beef
1 (8-oz.) cup tomato sauce
1 cup cooked rice
1 teaspoon chili powder
½ teaspoon salt
  Dash pepper
½ cup shredded Cheddar cheese

Place onions and water in 2-quart casserole. Cover. Cook on High for 8 to 9 minutes or until onions are just about tender. Drain. Scoop out centers of onions, leaving walls about ⅓-inch thick. Chop enough onion pulp to make ½ cup. Combine with ground beef in 1-quart casserole. Cook, covered, on High for 3 to 4 minutes. Drain off fat. Stir in half tomato sauce and all remaining ingredients except cheese. Stuff onions with beef-rice mixture, mounding high on top. Spoon any remaining mixture in dish around onions. Pour remaining tomato sauce over all. Cook on High 6 minutes. Sprinkle cheese on top. Continue to cook on High for 1 to 2 minutes or until cheese melts. Makes 4 servings.

LASAGNE INTERNATIONAL

    1 lb. Italian sausage, casings removed
    1 (16-oz.) can tomatoes, cut up
    1 (6-oz.) can tomato paste
    ¼ teaspoon dried basil, crushed
    ⅛ teaspoon garlic salt
   16 oz. ricotta or cottage cheese
    ¼ cup grated Parmesan cheese
    1 tablespoon chopped parsley
    1 egg, slightly beaten
    ½ teaspoon salt
    ⅛ teaspoon pepper
    1 (8-oz.) pkg. cooked lasagna noodles
    8 oz. mozzarella cheese, sliced

In 4-quart casserole, break up sausage and cook on High for 3 minutes, stirring once. Drain excess fat. Add tomatoes, tomato paste, basil and garlic salt. Cook, uncovered, on High for 10 minutes, stirring twice. In mixing bowl, stir together ricotta or cottage cheese, Parmesan cheese, parsley, egg, salt and pepper. Spoon a little meat sauce into bottom of 7½" x 12" utility dish. Arrange half the cooked noodles over sauce, then half the ricotta or cottage-cheese mixture, half the mozzarella cheese and half the meat sauce. Repeat. Cover with plastic wrap. Cook on High for 4 minutes. Turn dish. Cook another 4 minutes. Let stand 10 minutes. Makes 6 to 7 servings.

MOCK LASAGNE

    1 qt. Basic Meat Sauce, page 150
    ½ teaspoon dried oregano leaves, crushed
    ¼ teaspoon dried thyme leaves, crushed
    ¼ lb. Monterey Jack cheese, thinly sliced
    1 cup cottage cheese
    6 oz. medium noodles, cooked and drained
    ¼ cup grated Parmesan cheese

Combine meat sauce with oregano and thyme. Spread ⅓ of the meat sauce in bottom of 7½" x 12" utility dish. Add in layers half the Jack cheese, half the cottage cheese and half the noodles. Repeat, using ⅓ more of the meat sauce, the remaining Jack cheese, cottage cheese and noodles. Spread with remaining meat sauce. Sprinkle with Parmesan cheese. Cover with wax paper. Cook on High for 4 minutes. Turn dish. Cook another 4 minutes. Let stand several minutes before serving. Makes 6 servings.

SPAGHETTI WITH MEAT SAUCE

1 lb. lean ground beef
1 medium onion, chopped
1 garlic clove, minced
1 (28-oz.) can tomatoes, cut up
½ cup chopped celery
½ cup water
¼ cup Burgundy wine
1 (6-oz.) can tomato paste
2 tablespoons chopped parsley
1 tablespoon brown sugar
1 teaspoon dried oregano leaves, crushed
1 teaspoon salt
¼ teaspoon dried thyme leaves, crushed
1 bay leaf
3 cups cooked spaghetti
   Parmesan cheese

In 4-quart casserole, crumble beef. Add onion. Cook on High for 4 minutes, stirring twice. Add remaining ingredients except spaghetti and cheese. Cover. Cook on High for 5 minutes. Stir. Cook 10 minutes, stirring once. Serve sauce over spaghetti. Sprinkle with cheese. Makes 4 to 5 servings.
   Variation: Place ingredients from garlic through brown sugar in blender and puree. Add this pureed sauce and remaining seasonings to meat mixture. Continue recipe.

BEEF AND CHEESE BAKE

1 lb. ground beef
2 (8-oz.) cans tomato sauce
  Salt and pepper
¼ cup chopped green onions
2 tablespoons chopped green pepper
½ cup dairy sour cream
½ cup cottage cheese
1 (3-oz.) pkg. cream cheese
1 (5½-oz.) pkg. Noodles Romanoff,
    prepared according to package directions

In 2-quart casserole cook beef on High for 4 minutes, stirring once to break up chunks of beef. Drain excess fat. Add tomato sauce, salt and pepper. Cook on High for 5 minutes. Combine onions, green pepper, sour cream and cheeses. In 7½" x 12" utility dish, layer half the noodles, all the cheese mixture and the remaining noodles. Top with meat-sauce mixture. Cover with wax paper. Cook on High for 10 minutes. Makes 6 servings.

BEEF-NOODLE CASSEROLE

2 cups cooked green noodles
¼ cup butter or margarine
¼ cup Parmesan cheese
2 tablespoons salad oil
¼ cup chopped onion
2 garlic cloves, crushed
1½ lbs. lean ground beef
½ cup water
2 tablespoons sherry wine
1 tablespoon Worcestershire sauce
2 beef-bouillon cubes
1 teaspoon salt
¼ teaspoon pepper
2 cups grated Gouda or Cheddar cheese
¼ cup grated Parmesan cheese

Place noodles in 7½" x 12" utility dish. Warm on High for 1½ minutes. Add butter or margarine and ¼ cup Parmesan cheese. Toss well. Combine oil with onion and garlic in 4-quart casserole. Cook on High for 3 minutes. Stir in beef. Cook on High for 4 minutes. Add water, sherry, Worcestershire sauce, bouillon cubes, salt and pepper. Cook on High for 3 minutes. Stir 1½ cups Gouda or Cheddar cheese into meat mixture. Pour into noodle-lined casserole. Cover with wax paper. Cook on High for 8 minutes. Sprinkle with remaining Gouda or Cheddar cheese and ¼ cup Parmesan cheese. Heat until bubbly hot. Makes 6 servings.

ITALIAN MACARONI AND CHEESE

2 cups (8-oz.) mostaccioli, cooked
    and drained
3 tablespoons butter
¾ cup chopped onion
⅓ cup chopped celery
1 or 2 garlic cloves, minced
2 (6-oz.) cans tomato paste
2 cups water
1 teaspoon basil, crushed
1 teaspoon oregano, crushed
2 teaspoons salt
½ teaspoon sugar
½ teaspoon pepper
⅔ cup grated Parmesan cheese
2 cups ricotta cheese (1-lb.)

Cook mostaccioli on cooktop according to package directions. Combine butter, onion, celery and garlic in 1½-quart casserole. Cook on High for 3 to 4 minutes, stirring occasionally. Add tomato paste, water and seasonings. Cover and bring to a boil on High for about 10 minutes. Uncover. Cook on High for an additional 5 minutes. In 2-quart oblong utility dish, spread a thin layer of sauce over the bottom. Sprinkle with ⅓ of Parmesan cheese. Soften ricotta cheese on Low for 1 to 2 minutes. Layer with half each of mostaccioli, ricotta cheese, sauce and half of remaining Parmesan cheese. Repeat layers. Bake on Medium for 20 to 25 minutes or until hot and bubbly, rotating ½ turn after 10 minutes. Raise shelf. Brown 3 to 5 minutes until golden brown. Makes 6 servings.

CONFETTI MEATBALL SUPPER

  1 (10-oz.) pkg. frozen mixed
      vegetables
  3 cups cooked rice
  2 tablespoons melted butter or
      margarine
 24 Basic Meatballs, page 147
  ½ cup finely chopped onion
  1 (10¾-oz.) can condensed cream-
      of-mushroom soup
  1 (11-oz.) can condensed
      Cheddar-cheese soup
  ½ cup catsup
  2 tablespoons Worcestershire
      sauce

Pierce mixed-vegetable package and cook on High for 4 minutes. Drain. Mix with cooked rice and butter or margarine. Press into 5½-inch ceramic ring mold. In 7½" x 12" utility dish, cook meatballs and onion on High for 5 minutes. Drain excess fat. Mix soups, catsup and Worcestershire sauce. Pour over meatballs. Cover with wax paper. Cook on High for 10 minutes. Unmold rice ring on ceramic serving platter. Cover with wax paper. Heat on High 4 minutes. Arrange meatballs around rice mold. Pour some of sauce over meatballs and rice. Pass remaining sauce. Makes 6 servings.

NEW ENGLAND MEAT PIE

1 lb. lean ground beef
1 egg, slightly beaten
¼ cup fine, dry bread crumbs
2 tablespoons milk
1 teaspoon salt
1 (10-oz.) pkg. frozen mixed
    vegetables, partially thawed
¼ teaspoon thyme
¼ teaspoon pepper
1 (8-oz.) can tomato sauce
1 (12-oz.) pkg. frozen hash-brown
    potatoes, thawed
2 tablespoons salad oil
¼ cup grated cheese

Combine beef with egg, bread crumbs, milk and salt. Shape into 1-inch balls. Place on metal rack in 7½" x 12" utility dish. Cover. Cook on High for 5 minutes. Drain. Combine with vegetables, thyme, pepper and tomato sauce. Press potatoes on bottom and sides of regular 10-inch pie plate or deep 9-inch pie dish. Drizzle with oil. Heat on High for 3 minutes. Brown 5 minutes. Spoon meatball mixture over potatoes. Cook on High for 5 minutes. Sprinkle with cheese. Heat for 30 seconds. Makes 5 servings.

CORNED BEEF AND CABBAGE

3 lb.-round of corned beef in
    package with seasonings
3 medium potatoes, peeled and quartered
3 carrots, quartered
1 small head cabbage, cut into wedges

Place the corned beef and seasonings in large roasting bag tied with a string or rubber band. Set roasting bag inside 4-quart casserole. Cook on Low for 20 minutes. Turn dish. Cook a second 20 minutes. Open bag, add potatoes and carrots, close bag. Cook on Low for a third 20 minutes. Add cabbage to bag. Cook on Low for 15 minutes or until vegetables are tender. Let stand covered for 10 minutes. Makes 6 servings.

RUTH'S SHELL CASSEROLE

1 lb. lean ground beef
1 small onion, chopped
¼ cup flour
1 teaspoon salt
1 teaspoon Worcestershire sauce
¼ teaspoon garlic powder
1 (10½-oz.) can beef-bouillon soup
1 (2-oz.) can sliced mushrooms,
    drained
2 cups cooked large shell-shaped
    macaroni
1 cup dairy sour cream
2 tablespoons red wine
    Finely chopped parsley

In 4-quart casserole, break up beef with fork. Add onion. Cook on High for 4 minutes. Stir in flour, salt, Worcestershire sauce and garlic powder. Mix well. Add soup, mushrooms and cooked macaroni. Cover. Cook on High for 5 minutes, stirring once. Add sour cream and wine. Heat on High for 1 to 1½ minutes. Sprinkle with parsley. Makes 4 to 5 servings.

SWEDISH CABBAGE ROLLS

12 large cabbage leaves
2 tablespoons water
1 egg
⅔ cup milk
¼ cup finely chopped onion
1 teaspoon Worcestershire sauce
1 lb. lean ground beef
¾ cup cooked rice
1 (10½-oz.) can condensed tomato soup
¼ cup catsup
1 tablespoon brown sugar
1 tablespoon lemon juice

Place cabbage leaves in 4-quart casserole with 2 tablespoons water. Cover. Cook on High for 6 minutes. Set aside. In bowl, combine egg, milk, onion and Worcestershire sauce. Mix well, Add beef and rice to egg mixture and beat together with fork. Trim thick parts of cabbage leaves so you can roll them without tearing. Spoon ¼ cup of meat mixture on each leaf. Fold in sides and roll leaf ends over meat. Secure with toothpicks. Place rolls in 7½" x 12" utility dish. Combine soup, catsup, brown sugar and lemon juice. Pour over cabbage rolls. Cover with plastic wrap. Cook on High for 12 minutes. Let stand 5 minutes before serving. Makes 4 servings.

KNOCKWURST AND HOT GERMAN-POTATO SALAD

3 medium potatoes
4 slices bacon, diced
1 small onion, diced
1 tablespoon flour
1 tablespoon sugar
1 teaspoon dry mustard

1 teaspoon salt
¼ teaspoon pepper
½ cup water
¼ cup vinegar
½ teaspoon celery seeds
4 knockwurst
1 tablespoon finely chopped parsley

Wash potatoes; dry and cut in half. Place in plastic bag, cut side down. Leave end of bag open. Cook on High for 10 minutes or until tender. Remove skins and slice. Cook bacon and onion in 4-cup measure on High for 4 to 5 minutes. Stir in flour, sugar, mustard, salt and pepper. Mix well. Add water, vinegar and celery seeds. Cook on High another 4 minutes, stirring once. Set aside. Make several cuts in plastic bag containing knockwurst and place bag on paper plate. Cook on High for 1½ minutes. Cut each knockwurst into 6 pieces. Arrange knockwurst pieces and cooked potatoes in shallow bowl. Add hot sauce. Toss to coat evenly. Sprinkle with chopped parsley. Serve immediately. Makes 4 servings.

BEEF STROGANOFF

¼ cup butter or margarine
1½ lbs. beef sirloin, cut in ½" x 2" strips
¼ cup flour
1 beef-bouillon cube
¾ cup boiling water
1 small onion, chopped
¼ lb. fresh mushrooms, sliced
2 tablespoons tomato paste
1 teaspoon Worcestershire sauce
¾ teaspoon salt
1 cup dairy sour cream, room
    temperature

In 4-quart casserole, melt butter or margarine on High for 40 seconds. Coat beef with flour, then with melted butter or margarine. Cook, uncovered, on High for 3 minutes. Stir. Cook another 2 minutes. Dissolve bouillon cube in boiling water. Add bouillon, onion, mushrooms, tomato paste, Worcestershire sauce and salt to meat. Stir. Cover. Cook on High for 5 minutes. Let stand 4 minutes. Uncover. Stir in sour cream. Heat on High for 1 to 1½ minutes. Makes 4 servings.

STAG CHILI

1 lb. ground beef
½ cup chopped green pepper
1 tablespoon instant onion
2 (16-oz.) cans dark-red kidney
    beans, drained
1 (16-oz.) can tomatoes, cut up
1 (8-oz.) can tomato sauce
1 teaspoon seasoned salt
1 pkg. chili seasoning

In 4-quart casserole, cook meat, green pepper and onion on High for 5 minutes or until vegetables are tender, stirring once. Stir in remaining ingredients. Cover. Cook on High for 15 minutes, stirring once. Makes 6 servings.
   Variation: To make more spicy, substitute 2 (16-oz.) cans of chili beans with sauce for dark-red kidney beans.

CHILI STEAKS

2 tablespoons flour
1 teaspoon chili powder
1½ lbs. round steak, cut into 4 or 5 pieces
2 tablespoons salad oil

1 onion, sliced
1 (8-oz.) can tomatoes
1 (15-oz.) can chili with beans
1 teaspoon salt
½ cup grated Cheddar cheese

Combine flour and chili powder in plastic or paper bag. Pound meat and add to bag. Shake until coated. Pour oil in a 7½" x 12" utility dish. Heat on High for 1½ minutes. Add meat; turn to coat both sides with hot oil. Cook on High 4 minutes. Stir. Add onion, tomatoes, chili with beans and salt. Cover with wax paper. Cook on Low for 25 minutes, stirring once. Uncover; sprinkle with cheese. Cook on High for another 30 seconds. Makes 4 servings.

SPOONBURGERS

1½ lbs. lean ground beef
1 medium onion, chopped
1 (10½-oz.) can condensed tomato
     soup
2 tablespoons water
1 tablespoon vinegar
1 tablespoon brown sugar
1 teaspoon chili powder
1 teaspoon Worcestershire sauce
½ teaspoon salt
¼ teaspoon celery salt
5 or 6 hamburger buns

In 4-quart casserole, cook beef and onion on High for 6 minutes, stirring twice. Combine remaining ingredients except buns and pour over meat. Cover. Cook on High for 4 minutes. Warm all hamburger buns on Low for 1½ minutes. Spoon sauce over buns and serve. Makes 4 to 5 servings.

TACOS

1 lb. lean ground beef
1 (1¼-oz.) pkg. taco-seasoning mix
½ cup hot water
6 or 7 cooked taco shells
2 cups shredded lettuce
2 medium tomatoes, chopped
  Grated cheese

In 2-quart casserole, crumble beef. Cook on High for 4 minutes, stirring once. Drain fat; stir in dry taco-seasoning mix and water. Cover lightly with paper towel. Cook on High for 5 minutes, stirring once. Heat cooked taco shells on paper towel or paper plate on High for 30 seconds. Fill shells with ground-beef mixture, lettuce, tomatoes and cheese. Makes 6 to 7 tacos.

ORIENTAL SUPPER

24 Basic Meatballs, page 147
 1 (10½-oz.) can condensed beef broth
 1 soup-can hot water
 1 medium onion, sliced
1½ cups bias-sliced celery (½-inch pieces)
 1 (16-oz.) can chop-suey vegetables, drained
 1 (6-oz.) can mushrooms
 3 tablespoons cornstarch
 ½ cup cold water
 3 tablespoons soy sauce
 1 (3-oz.) can chow-mein noodles

In 7½" x 12" utility dish, cook meatballs on High for 5 minutes. Add beef broth and soup-can of hot water. Stir in onion and celery. Cover with wax paper. Cook on High for 8 minutes. Add chop-suey vegetables and mushrooms.

Blend cornstarch with ⅓ cup cold water and soy sauce. Stir into casserole. Cover. Cook on High for 5 minutes or until mixture thickens, stirring several times. Serve over chow-mein noodles. Makes 4 to 5 servings.

FIESTA BAKE

1 qt. Basic Meat Sauce, page 150
1 teaspoon chili powder
1 (12-oz.) can whole-kernel corn, not drained
1 (8½-oz.) pkg. corn-muffin mix
1 egg
⅓ cup milk
1 teaspoon sugar
   Chopped chives

Mix Basic Meat Sauce with chili powder and corn. Stir into 7½" x 12" utility dish. Cover with wax paper. Cook on High for 3 minutes. Uncover. In the meantime, combine muffin mix with egg, milk and sugar. Drop by tablespoon on top of hot meat-sauce mixture. Sprinkle with chives. Raise shelf. Cook on High for 5 minutes, turning dish once. Brown 3 to 5 minutes. Makes 6 servings.

HACIENDA HOLIDAY CASSEROLE

1 qt. Basic Meat Sauce, page 150
1 cup refried beans
2 tablespoons chopped green chiles
6 tortillas
1 (2¼-oz.) can sliced ripe olives, drained
2 cups grated Cheddar cheese

In 2-quart casserole, combine Basic Meat Sauce with re-fried beans and chiles. Arrange alternate layers of sauce with tortillas, olives and cheese. Cook on High for 7 minutes, turning casserole once. Makes 4 servings.

MANDARIN-STYLE STEAK

1½ lbs. round steak, about ½-inch thick
2   tablespoons salad oil
1   (1⅜-oz.) envelope onion-soup mix
2   tablespoons soy sauce
¼   teaspoon ground ginger
1   cup water
1   (8½-oz.) can water chestnuts,
      drained and sliced
½   green pepper, sliced
1   tomato, cut into wedges
2   tablespoons toasted sesame seeds

Cut steak into ¼-inch-wide strips. In 4-quart casserole, heat oil on High for 1½ minutes. Add meat. Cook on High for 3 minutes. Stir. Cook 1½ minutes. Stir in soup mix, soy sauce, ginger and water. Cover. Cook on Low for 25 minutes or until tender. Stir in water chestnuts, green pepper and tomato. Cook on High for 1 minute. Let stand 10 minutes before serving. Garnish with sesame seeds. Serve with crisp Chinese noodles. Makes 4 to 5 servings.

COUNTRY GARDEN BAKE

2   lbs. lean ground beef
1   garlic clove, crushed
1   cup chopped onion
    Salt and pepper
1   (10-oz.) pkg. frozen Mexican corn with butter sauce
1   (10-oz.) pkg. frozen peas in butter sauce
1   (3-oz.) can sliced mushrooms, drained
2   tablespoons butter or margarine
    Instant mashed potatoes, servings for 4
4   tablespoons grated Romano cheese
¼   cup grated Cheddar cheese

In 2-quart casserole, break up meat with fork. Add garlic and onion. Cook on High for 7 to 8 minutes. Sprinkle with salt and pepper. Pierce packages and thaw corn and peas in packages on High for 4 to 7 minutes. Add the corn, peas, mushrooms and butter or margarine to meat mixture. Stir until butter is melted. Cover. Cook on High for 6 minutes. While meat mixture is cooking, prepare instant potatoes according to package directions for 4 servings. Spoon potatoes over casserole. Raise shelf. Heat on High for 2 minutes. Sprinkle with cheeses. Brown 4 to 6 minutes. Makes 6 servings.

MEATBALL GARDEN DISH

24 Basic Meatballs, page 147
 1 (10½-oz.) can condensed beef broth
 1 soup-can hot water
 3 medium potatoes, peeled and quartered
 6 medium carrots, peeled,
      quartered and halved
 1 medium onion, sliced
 1 (10-oz.) pkg. frozen peas
⅓ cup flour
⅔ cup cold water
    Salt and pepper to taste

In 4-quart casserole, cook Basic Meatballs on High for 5 minutes, stirring once. Pour in broth and soup-can of hot water. Add potatoes, carrots and onion. Cover. Cook on High for 15 to 20 minutes or until vegetables are tender. With slotted spoon remove meat and vegetables and place in serving dish. Thaw peas in pierced package on High for 4 minutes. Add to meat and vegetable mixture. Stir flour into drippings left in 4-quart casserole. Add cold water and salt and pepper to taste. Cook on High for 5 minutes or until gravy thickens, stirring often. Pour part of gravy over vegetables and meat. Pass remainder. Makes 6 servings.

PIZZA BURGERS

2 lbs. lean ground beef
½ cup grated mozzarella cheese
¼ cup chopped ripe olives
2 tablespoons grated Parmesan cheese
1 teaspoon instant minced onion
½ teaspoon salt
1 (8-oz.) can pizza sauce
½ teaspoon oregano
½ teaspoon garlic salt

Divide meat into 4 large patties about 6-inches in diameter. Combine mozzarella, olives, Parmesan cheese, onion and salt. Place ¼ of cheese mixture in center of each burger. Fold burgers over; press edges together. Place on metal rack in 7½" x 12" utility dish. Cook on High for 4 minutes. Turn dish. Cook for 2 minutes. Rearrange meat on rack. Cook 2 to 4 minutes, depending on desired doneness. In 2-cup measure, combine pizza sauce with oregano and garlic salt. Heat on High for 3 minutes. Serve with burgers. Makes 4 generous servings.

BEEF ENCHILADAS WITH CHEESE

1 lb. lean ground beef
1 cup grated Monterey Jack or
     Cheddar cheese
1 (2½-oz.) can sliced ripe olives,
     drained
1 (6-oz.) can tomato paste
1 (1⅜-oz.) pkg. enchilada-sauce mix
3 cups warm water
8 corn tortillas
1½ cups grated Monterey Jack or
     Cheddar cheese

In 2-quart casserole, crumble beef. Cook on High for 4 minutes, stirring twice. Drain fat. Add 1 cup cheese and olives to meat. In 2½-quart casserole, blend tomato paste with enchilada-sauce mix. Stir in water. Cover. Cook on High for 8 minutes. Pour 1 cup prepared enchilada sauce in 7½" x 12" utility dish. Dip each tortilla into remaining heated sauce. Spoon meat mixture in center of each tortilla. Fold sides of tortilla over filling and place in baking dish, seam side down. Pour remaining sauce over filled tortillas. Top with 1½ cups cheese. Cover with plastic wrap. Heat on High for 3 minutes. Turn dish. Cook another 3 minutes. Makes 8 enchiladas.

VEGETABLES

CORN BAKE

2 (12-oz.) cans whole-kernel corn,
   drained
1 (6-oz.) can evaporated milk
1 egg, beaten
1 tablespoon minced onion
1 tablespoon diced pimiento
½ cup shredded Monterey Jack or
   Cheddar cheese
½ teaspoon salt
1 tablespoon butter
½ cup soft bread crumbs
¼ cup shredded Monterey Jack or
   Cheddar cheese

In 7½" x 12" utility dish, combine corn and milk with egg, onion, pimiento, ½ cup cheese and salt. In 1-cup measure, melt butter on High for 35 seconds. Stir in bread crumbs and ¼ cup cheese. Set aside. Cover casserole with wax paper. Raise shelf. Cook on High for 3 minutes. Turn dish. Cook another 2 minutes. Sprinkle with crumb topping. Heat 1 minute. Remove paper. Brown 5 minutes. Makes 6 servings.

HARVARD BEETS

2 tablespoons butter or margarine
¼ cup sugar
1 tablespoon cornstarch
¼ teaspoon salt
¼ cup vinegar
¼ cup beet juice, drained from canned beets
2 cups canned shoestring, cubed or
    sliced beets, drained

In 2-quart casserole, melt butter or margarine on High for 1 minute. Mix sugar and cornstarch together. Add salt. Stir into melted butter until smooth. Add vinegar and beet juice. Cook on High for 2 to 3 minutes, or until clear. Add drained beets. Cover. Heat on High for 4 minutes. Makes 4 servings.

PICKLED BEETS AND EGGS, CRACKER-BARREL STYLE

5 fresh beets
½ cup water
½ cup vinegar
½ cup cold water

¼ cup brown sugar, firmly packed
½ teaspoon salt
1 small stick cinnamon
3 whole cloves
6 hard-cooked eggs, peeled

Wash beets and trim stocks. Place beets in 2-quart casserole and add water. Cover. Cook on High for 12 minutes. Let stand, covered, while making sauce. Measure vinegar and cold water into 2-cup measure. Add brown sugar, salt, cinnamon and cloves. Drain beets. Slip off skins. Pour sauce over beets. Cover. Cook on High for 8 minutes. Let stand several days. Remove beets from sauce. Add eggs to sauce. Cover. Let pickle in refrigerator for 2 days before using. Makes 5 pickled beets and 6 pickled eggs.

CHILLED ASPARAGUS VINAIGRETTE

1 lb. fresh asparagus spears
¼ cup water

Sauce:
   Cooking liquid from asparagus
      spears with water to make ½ cup liquid
¼ cup cider vinegar
2 teaspoons parsley
2 teaspoons chives
2 teaspoons pimiento
2 teaspoons capers
1 teaspoon salt
½ teaspoon dry mustard
⅛ teaspoon pepper

Cut off or snap off the lower part of spears. If desired, peel spears with vegetable peeler. Place in rectangular baking dish, alternating the direction of half the spears. Add ¼ cup water. Cover with plastic wrap. Cook on High for 4 minutes. Rearrange spears, moving the inside ones to the outside of dish. Cook on High for 3 minutes. Drain. Reserve liquid for sauce. Prepare sauce and pour over asparagus spears. Place in refrigerator to marinate 12 hours or overnight. To serve, drain off liquid, reserving the parsley, chives, capers and pimientos as garnish. Makes 4 servings.

Sauce: Put all the ingredients in a screw-top jar. Cover jar tightly. Shake to blend well. Makes about ¼ cup.

Variation: Use 1 (10-oz.) package of frozen asparagus instead of fresh, if desired.

GREEN BEANS SUPREME

2 tablespoons butter or margarine
2 tablespoons flour
1 tablespoon instant minced onion
¼ teaspoon salt
½ teaspoon grated lemon peel
¼ teaspoon pepper
¼ cup water
1 cup dairy sour cream, room
    temperature
2 (16-oz.) cans green beans, drained
2 tablespoons butter or margarine
½ cup dry bread crumbs
¼ cup grated Cheddar cheese

In 4-cup measure, melt 2 tablespoons butter or margarine on High for 30 seconds. Stir in flour, onion, salt, lemon peel and pepper. Cook on High for 1 minute. Stir in water, then sour cream. Mix with green beans. Spoon into 2-quart casserole. In 2-cup measure, melt 2 tablespoons butter or margarine on High for 30 seconds. Stir in bread crumbs and cheese. Set aside. Raise shelf. Cook casserole on High for 5 minutes. Sprinkle bread-crumb topping over casserole. Heat on High for 1 minute. Brown 4 minutes. Makes 6 to 7 servings.

MARIE'S TOMATO STACK-UPS

1 (10-oz.) pkg. frozen spinach or
      broccoli, drained and chopped
3 large tomatoes
¼ teaspoon salt
½ cup grated Swiss cheese
¼ cup minced onion

Make 2 knife slits on top of spinach or broccoli package.
Cook in package on High for 6 minutes. Set aside. Cut the
tomatoes in half. Sprinkle lightly with salt. Set aside ¼ cup
of the grated cheese. Combine remaining cheese, spinach
and onion. Place tomato halves in 7½" x 12" utility dish.
Mound vegetable mixture onto the tomatoes. Raise shelf.
Cook on High for 4 minutes. Sprinkle with cheese. Brown
5 minutes. Makes 6 servings.

BROCCOLI-ONION BOUQUETS

4 medium white onions
1 lb. broccoli
½ cup chicken stock
   Salt and pepper

Peel onions and cut 1-inch core from center. Wash and
trim broccoli. Use flowerettes. Place broccoli and cored
onions separately in the same casserole. Add chicken
stock. Cover. Cook on High for 6 minutes. Place broccoli
flowerettes in cored onions. After cooking, broccoli should
fit snugly in cored onions. Cover. Cook on High for 3 minutes. Sprinkle with salt and pepper. Makes 4 servings.

SPINACH-CHEESE BAKE

1 (10-oz.) pkg. frozen chopped spinach
2 tablespoons flour
2 eggs, beaten
1 (3-oz.) pkg. cream cheese, cubed
¾ cup cubed American cheese
¼ cup butter, cubed
1½ teaspoons instant minced onion
½ teaspoon salt
½ cup fine bread crumbs
¼ cup butter
⅓ cup Parmesan cheese

In 1½-quart covered dish, cook spinach on High for 6 minutes, stirring once half-way through. Drain. Stir in flour, then eggs, cheeses, cubed butter, onion and salt. Mix well. Cook on High for 9 to 11 minutes, stirring twice. Remove from oven. Measure bread crumbs into a 1-cup measure. Add ¼ cup butter. Heat on High until butter is melted, about 1 minute. Stir until crumbs are well coated with butter. Sprinkle over the spinach mixture. Top with Parmesan cheese. Raise shelf. Brown as desired. Makes 4 servings.

CREAMY CABBAGE

¼ cup butter
½ small head cabbage, shredded, about 1 quart
¼ cup light cream
¼ teaspoon salt
¼ teaspoon seasoned salt
⅛ teaspoon pepper

In 2-quart casserole, melt butter on High for 40 seconds. Add cabbage, stirring to coat with butter. Cover. Cook on High for 2 minutes. Stir in cream. Cover. Cook on High for 3 minutes, stirring once. Sprinkle with salt, seasoned salt and pepper. Let stand several minutes before serving. Makes 4 servings.

SCALLOPED POTATOES

3 to 3½ cups raw boiling potatoes,
    peeled and thinly sliced
¾ cup grated Swiss cheese
½ cup milk
2 tablespoons butter or margarine
½ teaspoon onion salt
¼ teaspoon pepper

Butter 2-quart casserole. Place half of the potatoes in the casserole, top with half of the cheese, then the rest of the potatoes. In 2-cup measure, heat milk, butter or margarine and seasonings on High for 2 minutes. Pour over casserole. Raise shelf. Cover. Cook on High for 10 to 12 minutes or until crisp and tender. Top with remaining cheese. Remove cover. Brown 5 to 6 minutes. Makes 4 servings.

SUNSHINE POTATOES

¼ cup butter or margarine, melted
1 tablespoon fresh-squeezed lemon juice
3 large potatoes, thinly sliced
2 teaspoons fresh-grated lemon peel
3 tablespoons grated Parmesan cheese
½ teaspoon paprika

Combine melted butter or margarine and lemon juice. Arrange potato slices in 7½" x 12" utility dish. Brush cut surfaces of potatoes with lemon-butter mixture. Combine lemon peel, cheese and paprika. Sprinkle over potatoes. Raise shelf. Cover dish with plastic wrap. Cook on High for 10 to 12 minutes. Remove cover. Brown 5 to 6 minutes. Serve with lemon wedges. Makes 4 servings.

ORANGE-GLAZED SWEET POTATOES

3 large, cooked sweet potatoes or
    1 (29-oz.) can, drained
⅓ cup brown sugar, firmly packed
1 tablespoon cornstarch
⅓ cup orange juice
½ teaspoon grated orange peel
¼ teaspoon salt
2 tablespoons butter or margarine

Peel potatoes and cut into halves. If potatoes are large, cut into quarters. In 4-cup measure, combine sugar with cornstarch. Stir in orange juice, orange peel and salt. Cook on High for 2½ to 3 minutes, stirring twice. Add butter or margarine to glaze. If thinner glaze is desired, add more orange juice. Arrange potatoes in 2-quart casserole. Pour sauce over potatoes. Cook on High 5 to 6 minutes. Makes 4 to 5 servings.

Variations: Yams may be substituted for sweet potatoes. For marshmallow topping, sprinkle top of casserole with marshmallows after cooking. Raise shelf. Heat on High for 1 minute. Brown 3 to 5 minutes, turning dish once.

POTATOES AU GRATIN

4 medium potatoes
¼ cup butter or margarine
¼ cup flour
2 cups milk
½ teaspoon seasoned salt
⅛ teaspoon pepper
1 cup grated Cheddar cheese
1 onion, thinly sliced
½ cup grated Parmesan cheese
    Paprika

Wash potatoes. Dry and cut in half crosswise. Place in plastic bag, cut side down. Leave end of bag open. Cook on High for 10 minutes. Remove skins and slice. In 4-cup glass measure, melt butter or margarine on High for 40 seconds. Stir in flour, then milk, seasoned salt and pepper. Cook on High for 3½ minutes, or until mixture thickens, stirring twice. Blend in Cheddar cheese. Place cooked potatoes and onion in 7½" x 12" utility dish. Add sauce. Stir. Cover with wax paper. Raise shelf. Cook on High for 6 minutes. Exact cooking time depends on thickness of potatoes. Top with Parmesan cheese and paprika. Brown 5 minutes. Makes 4 servings.

TOMATOES PARMESAN

2 medium tomatoes
2 tablespoons grated Parmesan cheese
2 tablespoons fine, dry bread crumbs
1 tablespoon melted butter or margarine
1 teaspoon chopped chives
⅛ teaspoon paprika
   Dash of cayenne pepper

Cut tomatoes in half and place in 2-quart casserole. Combine the remaining ingredients and spoon over tomatoes. Raise shelf. Cook on High for 1½ to 2 minutes. Brown 4 to 5 minutes. Makes 4 servings.

GLAZED CARROTS

6 carrots, peeled and sliced crosswise
2 tablespoons water
2 tablespoons butter or margarine
¼ cup brown sugar, firmly packed
¼ teaspoon salt
1 teaspoon prepared mustard

In 2-quart casserole, cook carrots in water on High for 9 to 10 minutes, stirring twice. Drain, cover and set aside. In a 1-cup measure, melt butter or margarine on High for 30 seconds. Stir in brown sugar, salt and mustard. Pour over drained carrots. Cover. Heat on High for 2 minutes. Makes 4 servings.

STUFFED ZUCCHINI

  4 medium zucchini
  2 tablespoons water
  1 (6-oz.) pkg. chicken-flavored
       stuffing mix
1¾ cups water
  ¼ cup butter or margarine

In 7½" x 12" utility dish, place whole zucchini with 2 tablespoons water. Cover with wax paper. Cook on High for 10 to 12 minutes, turning dish once. Cool slightly. Cut in half, lengthwise. Scoop out centers and save. In 4-cup measure, combine seasoning packet from package of stuffing mix with 1¾ cup water and butter or margarine. Cook on High for 3 to 4 minutes. Cover and let stand 5 minutes. Stir in bread crumbs from mix to moisten. Add scooped-out zucchini centers. Spoon into cooked zucchini shells. Heat in 7½" x 12" utility dish on High for 4 to 6 minutes. Makes 8 servings.

MIXED VEGETABLE MEDLEY

  2 (10-oz.) pkgs. frozen, mixed
       vegetables
  3 tablespoons butter
  2 tablespoons flour
  1 cup light cream or milk
1½ teaspoons instant minced onion

Make two knife slits in top of vegetable package. Cook vegetables in package on High for 8 minutes. Drain and set aside. In 2-quart casserole, melt butter on High for 35 seconds. Blend in flour, then gradually stir in cream or milk. Cook on High for 1 minute. Stir. Cook 2 minutes. Add onion and drained vegetables. Makes 6 servings.

HOT BEAN TRIO

4 slices bacon
⅓ cup sugar
1 tablespoon cornstarch
1 teaspoon salt
¼ teaspoon pepper
½ cup white wine vinegar
1 onion, sliced
1 (1-lb.) can cut green beans, drained
1 (1-lb.) can cut wax beans, drained
1 (1-lb.) can kidney beans, drained
1 hard-cooked egg, sliced

Arrange bacon on metal rack in 7½" x 12" utility dish. Cover with paper towel. Cook on High for 4 minutes. Set bacon aside. Bacon crisps with standing time. Remove rack. Add sugar, cornstarch, salt, pepper, vinegar and onion to bacon drippings. Cook on High for 4 to 5 minutes or until thick, stirring several times. Add beans, mixing well. Cover. Cook on High 4 to 6 minutes, stirring once. Crumble bacon and sprinkle over top. Garnish with egg. Makes 8 to 9 servings.

QUICK BAKED BEANS

4 slices of bacon, diced
½ cup chopped onion
1 (28-oz.) can pork and beans
2 tablespoons brown sugar
1 tablespoon Worcestershire sauce
1 teaspoon prepared mustard

In 2-quart casserole, cook bacon and onion on High for 5 minutes. Drain excess fat. Add remaining ingredients. Cover. Cook on High for 8 to 10 minutes, stirring twice. Makes 5 to 6 servings.

SUMMER SQUASH ITALIANO

 3 tablespoons butter or margarine
 1 onion, minced
 1 garlic clove, minced
 1 small green pepper, chopped
   Oregano to taste
1½ lbs. summer squash, sliced
 4 medium tomatoes, peeled and chopped
 ½ teaspoon salt
 1 cup grated Parmesan cheese

In 7½" x 12" utility dish, cook butter or margarine with the onion, garlic, green pepper and oregano on High for 4 minutes. Stir in squash, tomatoes and salt. Cover. Raise shelf. Cook on High for 8 minutes. Stir and check for doneness. If necessary, cook 2 more minutes. Remove cover. Top with Parmesan cheese. Brown 4 to 5 minutes. Makes 6 servings.

GLAZED ACORN SQUASH

 2 acorn squash
 ½ cup honey
 1 tablespoon lemon juice
 ¼ teaspoon nutmeg
 ¼ teaspoon grated lemon peel

Pierce whole squash several times and place on paper towels. Cook on High for 8 to 10 minutes or until soft. Let stand 5 minutes. Slice crosswise into 1-inch slices. Scoop out seeds. Combine remaining ingredients. Place squash in

7½" x 12" utility dish. Spoon sauce over squash. Cover. Cook on High for 4 to 6 minutes or until hot. Makes 4 servings.

Variation: Squash may be cut in half lengthwise or in half crosswise.

ZUCCHINI AND MUSHROOMS GRATINÉ

4 medium zucchini, cut into 1-inch
  slices
2 tablespoons water
½ teaspoon dried dill
1 garlic clove
½ lb. fresh mushrooms, sliced
¼ cup butter or margarine
2 tablespoons flour
1 cup dairy sour cream, room
  temperature
½ cup crumbled herb croutons
½ cup grated Cheddar cheese

In 4-quart casserole, combine zucchini with water, dill and garlic. Cover. Cook on High for 5 minutes. Stir in mushrooms. Cover. Cook on High for 4 minutes. Let stand, covered, while making sauce. In 7½" x 12" utility dish, melt butter or margarine on High for 40 seconds. Stir in flour. Discard garlic clove from zucchini. Drain, reserving 2 tablespoons liquid. Add reserve liquid to flour and butter or margarine mixture. Stir. Cook on High for 2 minutes. Fold sour cream into sauce. Add zucchini and mushroom mixture. Cover with plastic wrap. Heat 4 minutes on High. Sprinkle with herb croutons and cheese. Remove plastic wrap. Raise shelf. Brown 4 to 5 minutes. Makes 5 to 6 servings.

SCALLOPED TOMATOES

3 tablespoons butter or margarine
¼ cup minced onion
¼ cup minced celery
1 tablespoon sugar
1 teaspoon salt
2 tablespoons flour
⅛ teaspoon pepper
1 (28-oz.) can tomatoes, cut up
3 slices bread, toasted, buttered and cut in cubes

In 2-quart casserole, place butter or margarine, onion and celery. Cover. Cook on High for 3 minutes. Add sugar, salt, flour and pepper. Cook on High for 1 minute. Stir in tomatoes. Cover. Cook on High for 3 minutes. Remove cover. Top with toast cubes. Cook on High 2 minutes more. Makes 4 servings.

RICE WITH VEGETABLES

1¾ cups water or stock
1   cup long-grain rice
3   tablespoons butter or margarine
½   teaspoon salt
2   small tomatoes, chopped, discard seeds
2   green onions, chopped
2   stalks celery, chopped
6   stuffed green olives, chopped

In covered 4-quart casserole heat water to boiling on High for 4½ minutes. Add rice, butter or margarine and salt. Cover. Cook on High for 10 to 11 minutes. With a fork, fold chopped vegetables into cooked rice. Let stand, covered, for 10 minutes. Makes 6 servings.

SAUCES

SHERRIED MEAT SAUCE

8 to 10 fresh mushrooms, sliced
2 tablespoons chopped green onions
1 teaspoon lemon juice
¼ teaspoon tarragon
¼ teaspoon pepper
  Drippings from beef roast or steak
2 tablespoons sherry

Add mushrooms, onions, lemon juice, tarragon and pepper to meat drippings. Cook on High for 2 minutes, stirring once. Pour hot sauce over meat. Warm sherry in a 1-cup glass measure or heat-resistant pitcher with handle on High for 30 seconds. Ignite with a match in the container for a spectacular serving finale. Be careful to hold your head away from the container opening when igniting.

BÉCHAMEL SAUCE

¼ cup butter or margarine
¼ cup flour
1 cup chicken broth or bouillon
1 cup light cream
½ teaspoon salt
  Dash of pepper and paprika

In 4-cup measure, melt butter on High for 40 seconds. Stir in flour. Cook on High for 1 minute, stirring once. Pour in broth, cream, salt, pepper and paprika. Cook on High for 3 minutes, stirring once every minute. Serve over chicken, seafood or vegetables. Makes about 2 cups of sauce.

CHEESE SAUCE

2 tablespoons butter
2 tablespoons flour
½ teaspoon salt
1 cup milk
½ cup grated sharp Cheddar cheese
   Salt and pepper to taste

In 4-cup glass measure, melt butter on High for 30 seconds. Stir in flour and salt. Mix well. Add milk. Cook, uncovered, on High for 2 minutes, stirring after 1 minute. Add cheese and stir until well blended. Cook, uncovered, on High for 2 more minutes or until creamy, stirring twice. Salt and pepper to taste. Pour over hot vegetable. Makes 1¼ cups of sauce.

HOLLANDAISE SAUCE

¼ cup butter or margarine
1 tablespoon lemon juice, (approx. ½ lemon)
2 egg yolks, well beaten
¼ cup light cream
½ teaspoon dry mustard
¼ teaspoon salt

In 2-cup glass measure, melt butter or margarine on High for 40 seconds. Stir in lemon juice, then egg yolks and cream. Cook on High for 1 to 1½ minutes, stirring every 15 to 30 seconds. Add seasonings. Beat until smooth. Makes 1 cup of sauce.

CLARIFIED BUTTER

1 cup butter (2 sticks)

In 2-cup liquid measure, melt butter slowly on Low for 1½ to 2½ minutes or until completely melted and oil starts to separate, but butter has not started to bubble or cook. Let butter stand a few minutes. Skim off foam. Slowly pour off yellow oil and reserve. This is the clarified butter. Discard leftover whey. Makes approximately ⅔ cup.

BÉARNAISE SAUCE

¼ cup dry white wine
2 tablespoons white wine vinegar
1 tablespoon minced shallots or green onions
1 teaspoon dried tarragon, crushed
4 egg yolks, beaten
⅔ cup clarified butter
¼ teaspoon salt
   White pepper to taste
   Dash cayenne

In 2-cup liquid measure, combine wine, vinegar, shallots or onions and tarragon. Bring to boil on High and continue cooking until about half of liquid is evaporated, 4 to 5 minutes. Strain liquid. Slowly pour hot strained liquid into egg yolks in a 1½-quart casserole, beating constantly with a wire whisk. Cook on Low for 1 to 2 minutes, stirring with a wire whisk after 30 seconds, then every 15 seconds until sauce is consistency of mayonnaise. Gradually beat in clarified butter. Season with salt, pepper and cayenne. Cover and set dish in bowl of hot, not boiling, water to keep warm. Makes about 1 cup sauce.

BARBECUE SAUCE

1 (8-oz.) can tomato sauce
¼ cup vinegar
2 tablespoons brown sugar
1 teaspoon prepared mustard
1 tablespoon Worcestershire sauce
1 tablespoon instant minced onion
¼ teaspoon salt
⅛ teaspoon liquid smoke

In 4-cup measure, combine all ingredients. Cover with plastic wrap. Cook on High for 5 minutes, stirring once. Let stand several minutes. Serve with ribs, chicken, chops, hamburger. Makes 1¼ cups.

CREOLE SAUCE

½ cup chopped onion
¼ cup chopped green pepper
¼ cup chopped celery
2 tablespoons butter
1 fresh tomato, peeled and chopped
1 (8-oz.) can tomato sauce
1 (3-oz.) can mushrooms, not drained
¼ teaspoon salt
⅛ teaspoon garlic powder

In 2-quart bowl, combine onion, pepper, celery and butter. Cover. Cook on High for 4 minutes. Stir in remaining ingredients. Cover. Cook on High for another 5 minutes. Serve over fish or vegetables. Makes 2½ cups of sauce.

FRESNO FRUIT SAUCE

½ cup raisins
½ cup water
¼ cup currant jelly
½ cup orange juice
¼ cup brown sugar, firmly packed
1 tablespoon cornstarch
⅛ teaspoon allspice

In 4-cup measure, combine raisins with water, jelly and orange juice. Heat on High for 3 minutes or until jelly melts, stirring once. Mix sugar, cornstarch and allspice. Stir into raisin mixture. Cook on High for 1½ minutes, stirring every 30 seconds. Serve with baked ham, pork chops or duck. Makes 1½ cups of sauce.

SWEET-SOUR SAUCE

½ cup sugar
3 tablespoons cornstarch
1 cup chicken broth
½ cup vinegar
½ cup pineapple juice
2 teaspoons soy sauce
½ cup pineapple bits
½ green pepper, coarsely chopped

In 4-cup glass measure, blend sugar and cornstarch. Stir in the liquids. Cook on High for 8 minutes, stirring once or twice. Add pineapple bits and green pepper. Serve over meatballs. Makes about 2½ cups of sauce.

MEDIUM WHITE SAUCE

½ cup Basic Creamy-Sauce Mix, see below
1 cup water

In 4-cup measure, combine Basic Creamy-Sauce Mix and water. Cook on High for 4 minutes, stirring often. Use as sauce for chipped beef, cooked fish or vegetables. Makes 1 cup of sauce.

BASIC CREAMY-SAUCE MIX

1⅓ cups non-fat dried-milk powder
¾ cup flour
1 teaspoon salt
½ cup butter or margarine

In mixing bowl, stir together milk powder, flour and salt. With pastry blender, cut in butter or margarine until mixture resembles small peas. Refrigerate in tightly covered container. Makes enough sauce for 6 cups Medium White Sauce.

BORDELAISE SAUCE

3 tablespoons butter or margarine
1 tablespoon minced onion
3 tablespoons flour
1 cup beef broth or bouillon
2 tablespoons red wine
1 tablespoon lemon juice
½ teaspoon dried tarragon, crushed
1 teaspoon finely chopped parsley
⅛ teaspoon brown sauce for gravy

In 4-cup measure, melt butter with onion for 1 minute on High. Stir in flour. Cook on High for 1 minute, stirring once. Pour in broth or bouillon, wine, lemon juice, tarragon and parsley. Cook on High for 3 minutes, stirring once every minute. Add brown sauce. Serve with broiled steak or roast beef. Makes 1¼ cups of sauce.

BUTTER-CRUMB TOPPING

¼ cup butter or margarine
1 cup bread crumbs, soft or dry
¼ cup shredded Cheddar cheese
    (optional)

In 9-inch pie plate, melt butter or margarine on High for 40 seconds. Stir in bread crumbs and cheese if desired. Cook on High for 1 minute. Sprinkle over cooked broccoli, green beans or stewed tomatoes. Makes 2 to 4 servings.

BROWNED LEMON BUTTER

¼ cup butter or margarine
1 tablespoon lemon juice
   Dash Worcestershire sauce

In 9-inch pie plate, heat butter or margarine on top shelf with browning unit for 7 minutes or until golden. Cool slightly. Stir in lemon juice and Worcestershire sauce. Serve over cooked vegetables or fish. Makes 2 to 4 servings.

GRAVY

½ cup drippings (fat and juices from meat)
½ cup flour
4 cups liquid (broth, juices or water)
   Salt and pepper
   Brown sauce for gravy (optional)

Pour drippings in 7½" x 12" utility dish or 4-quart casserole. Stir in flour. Cook on High for 1 minute, stirring once. Pour in liquid, stirring until well blended. Cook on High 4 to 5 minutes or until thick, stirring several times. Season with salt and pepper. Add a few drops of brown sauce for a deeper brown color. Makes about 1 quart of gravy.

EGGS AND CHEESE

EGGS BENEDICT

4 halves toasted English muffins
4 slices cooked ham
2 cups water

1 teaspoon vinegar
4 eggs
   Hollandaise Sauce, page 210

Arrange muffin halves in 7½" x 12" utility dish. Top with ham. To poach eggs, place 2 cups of hot water in 2-quart covered casserole, cover and bring to a boil on High. Pierce the egg yolks with a toothpick or fork. Add vinegar and swirl water with spoon. Carefully slip eggs, one at a time, into the water. Cover. Cook on Low for 2 minutes. Remove eggs with slotted spoon and arrange 1 poached egg on each ham slice. Spoon Hollandaise Sauce over all. Cook on High for about 1 minute or until heated. Makes 4 servings.

CHEESE SOUFFLÉ

Sauce:
¼ cup all-purpose flour
¾ teaspoon dry mustard
¾ teaspoon salt
¼ teaspoon paprika
⅛ teaspoon cayenne pepper
1 (13-oz.) can evaporated milk
2 cups lightly packed, grated sharp
   Cheddar cheese

Soufflé:
6 eggs, separated
1 teaspoon cream of tartar

Sauce: In 4-cup measure, add flour, dry mustard, salt, paprika and cayenne pepper. Slowly add evaporated milk and mix together until smooth. Cook on High for 3 or 4 minutes or until sauce thickens. Stir after 2 minutes, then every 30 seconds. Add cheese and mix until cheese is melted. Set aside.

Soufflé: In large mixing bowl, beat egg whites and cream of tartar with electric mixer until stiff, but not dry. In a medium bowl, beat egg yolks until thick and lemon-colored. Gradually add cheese sauce to egg yolks until thoroughly blended. Fold mixture carefully into beaten egg whites. Put into ungreased 2-quart soufflé dish. Cook on Low for 18 to 20 minutes or until top is dry, giving dish a quarter turn every 5 minutes. Serve immediately. Makes 6 servings.

CREAMY SCRAMBLED EGGS

6 eggs
¼ cup milk
¼ teaspoon salt
   Dash pepper
2 tablespoons butter or margarine
1 (3-oz.) pkg. cream cheese, cut in
   ½-inch cubes
   Chopped chives

Mix eggs with milk, salt and pepper. In 2-quart casserole, melt butter or margarine on High for 30 seconds. Pour in egg mixture. Cook on Low for 6 minutes, stirring occasionally the last 3 minutes of cooking. Add cream-cheese cubes. Cook on Low for 45 to 60 seconds. Sprinkle with chives. Makes 4 servings.

CORN PUDDING

   One bunch green onions, chopped
¼ cup chopped green pepper
4 to 6 tablespoons butter
3 eggs, beaten
5 cups canned corn, drained, or kernels
   from 5 or 6 ears fresh corn
¾ cup mocha mix
3 tablespoons sugar
2 tablespoons flour
½ teaspoon salt

In 2-quart covered casserole, partially cook onions, green pepper and butter on High for 3 minutes. Mix the remaining ingredients together and add to the onion-green-pepper mixture. Stir. Cover. Cook on Low for 20 minutes, turning dish a half turn after 10 minutes. Remove cover. Raise shelf. Brown 5 to 6 minutes. Makes 6 to 8 servings.

BREADS AND CEREALS

WHOLE-WHEAT BANANA BREAD

½ cup butter or margarine
1 cup sugar
2 eggs, slightly beaten
1 cup (about 3 medium) mashed
   bananas
1 cup white, all-purpose flour
1 cup whole-wheat flour
1 teaspoon soda
½ teaspoon salt
⅓ cup hot water
½ cup chopped walnuts

Melt butter or margarine on High for 45 seconds. Blend in sugar. Mix with beaten eggs and bananas until smooth. Sift white flour; measure. Sift again with whole-wheat flour, soda and salt. Add dry ingredients to banana mixture alternately with hot water. Stir in nuts. Line 9" x 5" loaf dish with wax paper. Pour batter into dish. Cook on Medium for 18 to 19 minutes, giving dish a quarter turn 3 times. Brown 4 to 5 minutes. Let cool for 10 minutes. Remove from dish and cool completely. Makes 1 loaf.

PILGRIM'S PUMPKIN BREAD

1½ cups sugar
1½ cups flour
 1 teaspoon salt
 1 teaspoon soda
 1 teaspoon cinnamon
 ½ teaspoon nutmeg
 ¼ teaspoon cloves
 ½ cup salad oil
 ⅓ cup water
 2 eggs
 1 cup canned pumpkin
 ½ cup chopped walnuts
 ½ cup chopped pitted dates

In large mixing bowl, combine all dry ingredients. Using an electric mixer, add the oil, water, eggs and pumpkin. Mix only until thoroughly blended, about 1 minute. Fold the nuts and dates into the batter. Pour into a greased 10-cup ring mold that has been sprinkled with cinnamon. Cook on Medium for 13 to 15 minutes, turning twice. If you do not have a plastic or ceramic 10-cup ring mold or Bundt dish, divide the batter in half and bake in a greased 1½-quart loaf dish. Cool 10 minutes. Makes 2 loaves.

DATE-NUT BREAD

 ¾ cup water
 ¾ cup finely chopped dates
 2 tablespoons shortening
 1 egg
1¼ cups flour
 ¼ cup brown sugar, firmly packed
 ½ teaspoon soda
 ½ teaspoon salt
 ½ teaspoon cinnamon
 ¼ teaspoon nutmeg
 ½ cup chopped nuts

Heat water to boiling and pour over dates. Stir to break dates apart. Add shortening so it will melt. Let cool to room temperature. Beat egg and add to date mixture. Sift dry ingredients together. Add date mixture to dry ingredients, stirring only until mixed. Stir in nuts. Pour into greased 8¼" x 5¼" x 2¼" loaf dish. Bake on Medium for 7½ to 8½ minutes. Give dish a half turn after 4 minutes. Bread is done when toothpick inserted in center comes out clean. Allow to cool 10 minutes before removing from dish to cooling rack. Makes 1 loaf.

CHILI-CHEESE CORN BREAD

2 eggs
1 cup sour cream
1 (8-oz.) pkg. corn-bread mix
1 (8-oz.) can whole-kernel corn, drained
1 (4-oz.) can diced green chiles, drained
1 cup grated Monterey Jack cheese

Grease an 8½-inch ceramic ring mold. Blend eggs, sour cream and mix. Stir in drained corn. Pour half the batter into ring mold. Sprinkle on chiles and half the cheese. Pour on remaining batter and top with cheese. Cover with plastic wrap. Raise shelf. Bake on Medium for 5 minutes. Turn dish and remove plastic wrap. Cook on Medium for 4 to 5 minutes. Brown 4 minutes. Makes 9 servings.

MAKE-YOUR-OWN TOASTED CEREAL

⅓ cup chopped blanched almonds
1 cup quick-cooking rolled oats
⅓ cup wheat germ
⅓ cup raisins
⅓ cup chopped dried apples or
    apricots
¼ cup brown sugar, firmly packed

Combine almonds, rolled oats and wheat germ. Spread in 7½" x 12" utility dish. Raise shelf. Brown for 10 minutes, stirring occasionally. Remove from heat. Stir in raisins, apples or apricots and brown sugar. Store in refrigerator. Serve with milk or cream. Makes about 2½ cups.

CALORIE COUNTERS

ITALIAN CHICKEN

1½ lbs. chicken breasts, boned, skinned and halved
¼ cup salad oil
1 garlic clove, minced
1 medium onion, thinly sliced separated into rings
1 (8-oz.) can chicken consommé
½ lb. fresh mushrooms, sliced

Cut breasts into quarters. Remove skin. Preheat browning dish on High for 7 minutes. Add oil, garlic and chicken pieces, meaty side down. Cook on Medium for 3 minutes. Turn chicken over. Cook on Medium for 3 minutes more. Remove chicken from dish and set aside. Add onions and consommé to dish. Cook on High for 3 minutes. Add chicken and cover dish. Cook on Medium for 15 minutes. Add mushrooms and cover. Cook on Medium for 5 minutes. Makes 3 servings.

CHICKEN CACCIATORA

2 lbs. chicken breasts
    Seasoned salt
1 to 1½ cups sliced mushrooms
2 cups stewed tomatoes
2 small green peppers, chopped

2 tablespoons finely chopped pimiento
3 teaspoons dried parsley
1 teaspoon salt
¼ teaspoon dried thyme
1 clove garlic, pressed
1 bay leaf
 Pepper to taste

Place chicken pieces in a 7½" x 12" utility dish. Sprinkle lightly with seasoned salt and top with mushrooms. In a 4-cup measure, combine remaining ingredients. Cook on High for 5 minutes or until mixture comes to a boil. Pour over chicken and mushrooms. Cover. Cook on Medium for 20 minutes. Makes 4 servings.

CHICKEN SURPRISE

2 lbs. chicken breasts, skinned and halved
1 garlic clove, minced
½ teaspoon ground oregano
3 cups tomato juice

In 2-quart casserole, place the chicken breasts, meaty side up. Sprinkle with garlic and oregano. Pour tomato juice over chicken and cover. Cook on Medium for 40 minutes. Rearrange chicken. Cook on Medium for another 10 minutes or until chicken is done and the juice thickened. Makes 6 servings.

MEATBALL SOUP

2 lbs. lean ground beef or ground veal
1 (46-oz.) can tomato juice
2 (8-oz.) cans tomato sauce
½ teaspoon oregano
½ teaspoon salt
¼ teaspoon pepper
2 tablespoons instant minced onion
1 tablespoon garlic powder

1 tablespoon Worcestershire sauce
2 cups diced carrots
2 cups diced celery
1 cup diced zucchini
1 cup sliced fresh mushrooms

Form meat into walnut-size meatballs. Place in 3-quart shallow casserole. Cook on High for 8 minutes. Rearrange the meat in the dish carefully so the meatballs will not be broken. Drain fat and set aside. In 4½-quart bowl, combine tomato juice, tomato sauce and all the spices. Bring to a boil on High. Add the carrots, celery and zucchini. Cover. Cook on High for 10 minutes or until soft. Add the mushrooms and cover. Cook on High for 5 minutes. Add the meat to the tomato-vegetable mixture. Cover. Heat on High to serving temperature. Makes 8 servings.

SHRIMP SAUTÉ WITH BEAN SPROUTS

1 tablespoon olive oil
1 lb. green shrimp, shelled and
    deveined (washed and drained
    on several layers of paper towels)
1 garlic clove, minced
1 tablespoon finely minced chives
½ teaspoon ground ginger
½ cup water
1½ tablespoons instant chicken bouillon
1 lb. fresh bean sprouts, washed and drained
2 tablespoons soy sauce

Preheat the browning dish on High for 5 minutes. Quickly add the olive oil, shrimp, garlic, chives and ginger. Stir. Cook on Medium for 1 minute. Stir. Cook 1 minute longer or until shrimp are pink. In a 2-quart casserole make chicken broth by bringing to a boil the water and instant chicken-bouillon, about 1½ minutes on High. Add the drained bean sprouts. Cover. Cook on Medium for 4½ minutes. Add the bean sprouts and soy sauce to the shrimp. Cover. Cook on Medium for 1 minute. Makes 4 servings.

SWEETS

OLD-FASHIONED CARROT CAKE

1½ cups sugar
 1 cup oil
 1 teaspoon vanilla
 3 eggs
1½ cups unsifted flour
 ¾ teaspoon salt
2½ teaspoons cinnamon
1¼ teaspoons soda
2¼ cups grated raw carrots
 ½ cup chopped walnuts
 ½ cup raisins

In a large mixing bowl, mix sugar, oil and vanilla. Add eggs; beat well. Combine flour, salt, cinnamon and soda. Stir into egg mixture. Fold in carrots, walnuts and raisins. Pour batter into 12" x 7" baking dish which has been greased on bottom only. Cook on High for 14 to 16 minutes, giving dish one-half turn every 4 minutes. Cool. Frost with Cream-Cheese Frosting, see below. Makes one cake.

CREAM-CHEESE FROSTING

½ lb. powdered sugar
1 (3-oz.) pkg. cream cheese
3 tablespoons butter
1 teaspoon vanilla

Place sugar in 2-quart casserole. Add cream cheese, butter and vanilla. Cook on High for 1 minute, just until ingredients can be beaten together. Beat with electric mixer until fluffy. Makes enough to frost 7" x 12" cake.

GRASSHOPPER PIE

¼ cup butter
16 to 18 chocolate cookies with
    vanilla-creme filling, crushed
35 large marshmallows (about 8 oz.)
½ cup milk
¼ cup green creme de menthe
¼ cup white creme de cacao
1 cup whipping cream

In 9-inch pie plate, melt butter on High for 40 seconds. Add crushed cookies and mix well. Press mixture into bottom and sides of pie plate to form shell. Cook on High for 1½ to 2 minutes. Set aside and cool. In 2-quart bowl, heat marshmallows and milk on High for 2 to 2½ minutes or until marshmallows are puffy and begin to melt. Stir well until marshmallows are completely melted. Cool several minutes. Stir in liqueurs. Cool until partially thickened. Whip cream; fold into marshmallow mixture. Spoon into cookie-lined pie plate. Refrigerate until firm. Garnish with additional whipped cream and chocolate curls if desired. Makes 6 to 8 servings.

CREAMY CHEESE PIE

Crust:
1 cup graham-cracker crumbs
¼ cup melted butter or margarine

Filling:
2 eggs, well beaten
1 (8-oz.) pkg. cream cheese,
    softened
½ cup sugar
⅛ teaspoon salt
1 teaspoon vanilla
⅛ teaspoon almond flavoring
1½ cups dairy sour cream
    Cinnamon

Crust: Mix graham-cracker crumbs with butter. Press on sides and bottom of 9-inch pie plate.

Filling: In mixing bowl, combine eggs with cream cheese, sugar, salt, vanilla and almond flavoring. Beat until smooth. Stir in sour cream. Cook on Low for 10 minutes, stirring every 2 minutes. Pour into baked crumb crust. Cook cheesecake on Low for 3 minutes. Rotate dish a quarter turn and continue cooking 1 to 3 minutes or until center is set. Chill several hours before serving. Serve plain, or sprinkle with cinnamon, or top with prepared fruit-pie filling. Makes 6 to 8 servings.

CHERRY COBBLER

1 (21-oz.) can prepared cherry-pie filling
¾ cup flour
2 tablespoons sugar
1 teaspoon baking powder
⅛ teaspoon salt
3 tablespoons butter softened
2 tablespoons milk
1 egg, slightly beaten

Pour pie filling into 8¼-inch, shallow, round baking dish. Combine flour with sugar, baking powder and salt. Cut in butter until mixture resembles coarse crumbs. Mix milk with egg. Add to dry mixture, stirring just to moisten. Spoon topping over fruit in 5 mounds. Cook on Medium for 6 minutes, turning baking dish several times. Brown for 4 to 5 minutes. Makes 5 servings.

PEACH SOUFFLÉ

2 cups hot water
1 (3-oz.) pkg. orange-flavored gelatin
1 (3-oz.) pkg. peach-flavored gelatin
2 (10- to 12-oz.) pkgs. frozen peaches in syrup
1¼ cups syrup drained from
    peaches; add water if necessary
1 (8-oz.) pkg. cream cheese
2 cups (1 pt.) whipping cream

In 2½-quart casserole bring hot water to a boil on High for 4 to 5 minutes. Add gelatins, stirring to dissolve. Refrigerate. Remove frozen peaches from cardboard-metal containers, or snip plastic pouches and place in a glass bowl. Defrost on Medium for 3 to 4 minutes or until peaches can be broken apart. Stir once while defrosting. Drain syrup and reserve. Save some peaches for the top and chop remaining peaches into bite-size pieces. Remove cream cheese from foil wrapper and place in small mixing bowl. Soften on Low for 1 to 1½ minutes. Beat with an electric mixer. Gradually blend in peach syrup. Stir into gelatin mixture. Refrigerate until gelatin mounds (about 2 hours). Whip cream. Two cups cream will make 4 cups whipped cream. Reserve 1 cup whipped cream. Fold peaches and the other 3 cups whipped cream into gelatin. Pour into 6 individual soufflé dishes with ½-inch collars or one 5 to 6-cup soufflé dish with a 2-inch collar. Garnish with reserved peach slices and reserved cup of whipped cream. Makes 6 servings.

BAKED APPLES

4 medium cooking apples
4 tablespoons brown sugar
2 tablespoons butter
  Dash cinnamon or nutmeg

Core apples. Cut a strip of peel from the top of each. Place apples in 8-inch round cake dish. Press 1 tablespoon brown sugar into each hole. Add ½ teaspoon butter and a dash of cinnamon or nutmeg. Cook apples on Low for 5 minutes. Turn dish. Cook on Medium for 5 minutes. Place apples in serving dish. Pour any syrup left in the baking dish into the center of apples. Cool. Makes 4 servings.

BROWNIES

⅔ cup butter or margarine
1 cup sugar
2 eggs, slightly beaten
1 teaspoon vanilla

1 cup sifted all-purpose flour
¼ cup dry cocoa
¼ cup instant cocoa
½ teaspoon baking powder
½ cup chopped walnuts

Melt butter or margarine in bowl on High for 1 minute or until melted. Add sugar. Cool. Add eggs and vanilla. Sift flour, dry cocoa, instant cocoa and baking powder into sugar mixture and blend in. Stir in nuts. Pour into lightly greased 9-inch glass pie plate. Cook on High for 4½ to 5½ minutes, turning 3 times. Cool before cutting. Makes 1 dozen brownies.

QUICK PEACH BRÛLÉE

2 fresh peaches, peeled and halved or
      4 canned peach halves, drained
¾ cup dairy sour cream
1 tablespoon granulated sugar
¼ teaspoon grated lemon peel
¾ cup brown sugar, firmly packed

Arrange peach halves, cut side down, in 4 custard cups. Cook on High for 1 minute. Combine sour cream with granulated sugar and lemon peel. Spoon over fruit. Just before serving, sprinkle brown sugar over entire surface of sour cream. Raise shelf. Brown for 3 to 3½ minutes or until brown sugar begins to melt. Serve immediately. Makes 4 servings.

MERRY MINTS

3 cups granulated sugar
½ cup light corn syrup
⅔ cup water
¼ teaspoon salt
2 egg whites
¼ teaspoon vanilla
1 cup chopped nuts

In 3-quart bowl, cook sugar, syrup and water on High for 12 to 13 minutes until it spins a fine thread. Add salt to egg whites and beat them on high speed until stiff. Slowly pour syrup mixture in a thin stream into the egg whites, beating constantly until mixture loses its shine and thickens. Stir in vanilla and nuts. Drop by teaspoons at once on waxed paper. Makes about 30 pieces.

FANTASTIC FUDGE

4 cups sugar
1 (14-oz.) can evaporated milk
1 cup butter or margarine
1 (12-oz.) pkg. semi-sweet chocolate pieces
1 (7-oz.) jar marshmallow creme
1 teaspoon vanilla
1 cup chopped walnuts

In 4-quart bowl, combine sugar, milk and butter or margarine. Cook on High for 18 to 20 minutes or until mixture reaches soft-ball stage. Stir often while mixture is cooking. Watch carefully to avoid boiling over. Mix in chocolate and marshmallow creme. Stir until well blended. Add vanilla and nuts. Pour into buttered 9-inch square dish for thick pieces. For thinner pieces, use 7½" x 12" dish. Cool and cut into squares. Makes about 20 pieces.

PEACH MELBA

1 pkg. frozen raspberries
½ cup currant jelly
2 tablespoons cornstarch
2 tablespoons water
6 canned peach halves
  Vanilla ice cream

Place the raspberries in 1½-quart glass bowl. Thaw on Medium for 3 minutes. Mash berries with a spoon. Sieve to separate the seeds. Add the jelly and bring just to a boil. Add the cornstarch mixed with water and cook on High until clear and mixture thickens, stirring often with wire wisk. Chill. Place a canned peach half, cut side up, in each individual dessert dish. Top each with a scoop of ice cream and pout the cooled sauce over the top. Makes 6 servings.

INDEX